John Stevens

Power-Grammatik Englisch

Für Anfänger
zum Üben & Nachschlagen

Hueber Verlag

Beratung: Christine House

7. 6. 5. | Die letzten Ziffern
2011 10 09 08 07 | bezeichnen Zahl und Jahr des Druckes.
Alle Drucke dieser Auflage können, da unverändert,
nebeneinander benutzt werden.
1. Auflage

Umschlaggestaltung: Parzhuber & Partner, München
Zeichnungen: Martin Guhl, Duillier/Schweiz
Redaktion: Marion Kerner, Hueber Verlag, Ismaning
DTP: Satz+Layout Fruth GmbH, München
Druck und Bindung: Ludwig Auer GmbH, Donauwörth
Printed in Germany
ISBN 978-3-19-002719-4

Wenn Sie Lernende/r im Anfängerbereich sind oder die englische Grundgrammatik systematisch wieder aufarbeiten wollen, bietet Ihnen die Power-Grammatik Englisch ein übersichtliches Lern- und Übungsprogramm, mit dem Sie Ihr Ziel konsequent erreichen.

Die Power-Grammatik Englisch zeichnet sich durch folgende Merkmale aus:

multifunktional

Mit der Power-Grammatik Englisch können Sie nachschlagen, lernen und üben. Das Buch kann im Selbststudium oder auch kursbegleitend eingesetzt werden. Sie können sich je nach Bedarf einzelne Units oder zusammenhängende Grammatikthemen (wie die Vergangenheitsform oder Present Perfect, das Passiv oder die Relativsätze) auswählen oder auch systematisch das gesamte Buch bearbeiten.

übersichtlich

Jede Lerneinheit umfasst zwei Seiten und hat den gleichen überschaubaren Aufbau:

- linke Seite: Erklärungen und Beispiele – rechte Seite: Übungen
- Der Einstieg in das jeweilige Grammatikthema erfolgt über einen humorvollen und anschaulichen Cartoon, der die Verwendung und den Gebrauch illustriert.
- Die Beispielsätze sind zum besseren Verständnis alle übersetzt, die Regeln sind knapp und leicht verständlich formuliert. Unterschiede zum deutschen Sprachgebrauch werden besonders hervorgehoben.
- Die Übungen sind progressiv aufgebaut: Sie bearbeiten zuerst leichtere Übungen, anspruchsvollere stehen am Schluss.

umfassend

In 65 Units bewältigen Sie alle für Anfänger/innen wichtigen Strukturen der Grundgrammatik. Der Schwerpunkt liegt auf den englischen Zeiten (tenses).

kleinschrittig

Sie lernen in leichten Teilschritten: komplexere Themen sind über mehrere sorgfältig gestaffelte Units verteilt.

komplett

- Tests zur Erfolgskontrolle nach Abschluss aller großen Themenbereiche
- Anhang mit Lösungsschlüssel aller Übungen und Liste der unregelmäßigen Verben

effektiv

Die Power-Grammatik Englisch ist nach dem Prinzip Verstehen – Lernen – Üben – Testen aufgebaut. Sowohl innerhalb eines Themenbereichs als auch innerhalb einer Lerneinheit ist das Material progressiv aufgebaut. Sie erarbeiten die besonderen Lernprobleme Stück für Stück und erzielen damit einen optimalen Lernerfolg.

Inhalt

Einfache Gegenwart – Verlaufsform der Gegenwart

Vergangenheitsform (Simple Past) – Present Perfect

Inhalt

Zeitformen der Zukunft

Das Passiv

Fragen

Modalverben

Inhalt

some – any

Präpositionen

1 She eats seaweed.

Sie isst Seetang.

we eat – she eats

Die Bildung der englischen Verbformen macht (im Gegensatz zu deren Anwendung) nicht allzu große Probleme, weil es im Vergleich zum Deutschen nur wenige Endungen gibt. In dieser Unit geht es um die -s-Endung in der einfachen Gegenwart (Englisch: *simple present*)

[1] Seetang

Regel In der 3. Person Einzahl der einfachen Gegenwart hängen wir die Endung -s an das Verb: he / she / it – das „s" muss mit!

I / you / we / they	eat	he / she / it	eats

I **live** here. My brother **lives** in the USA. *Ich lebe hier. Mein Bruder lebt in den USA.*
We both **work**. Ann **works** from home. *Wir arbeiten beide. Ann arbeitet von zu Hause.*

Nach einem Zischlaut (sh, ch) wird die -s-Endung zu -es.

I / you / we / they	finish	teach	wash	watch
he / she / it	finishes	teaches	washes	watches
	beenden	*unterrichten*	*waschen*	*zusehen*

Nach einem Konsonanten wird -y + -s zu -ies.

I / you / we / they	fly	hurry	study	try
he / she / it	flies	hurries	studies	tries
	fliegen	*eilen*	*studieren*	*versuchen*

Aber: Nach einem Vokal bleibt -y vor -s unverändert: say – says (sagen), pay – pays (bezahlen).

Die Verben have, do und go haben besondere Formen.

I / you / we / they	have	do	go
he / she / it	**has**	**does**	**goes**
	haben	*tun, machen*	*gehen, fahren*

Die einfache Gegenwart (1)

he / she / it + -s

1. Kreuzen Sie die richtige Form an.

a I ... a lot of cheese.
- ☐ eat
- ☐ eats

b David ... red wine.
- ☐ like
- ☐ likes

c Karin and I ... work at 6.
- ☐ finish
- ☐ finishes

d Angela ... squash.
- ☐ play
- ☐ plays

e My son ... a lot of TV.
- ☐ watch
- ☐ watches

f They ... the *Süddeutsche Zeitung.*
- ☐ read
- ☐ reads

2. Ergänzen Sie die -s-Form des Verbs.

a A TV star ________________ in that house. *(live)*
b Dave ________________ French and Italian. *(speak)*
c He ________________ languages. *(teach)*
d My neighbour ________________ his car every week. *(wash)*
e Angela ________________ a dog and two cats. *(have)*
f She ________________ a Mini. *(drive)*

3. Ergänzen Sie die richtige Form des Verbs.

a The shops ________________ *(open)* at 9.30 in the morning.
b My train ________________ *(leave)* here at 7.30, and ________________ *(arrive)* in Munich thirty minutes later.
c We ________________ *(know)* a lot of people through our children.
d My colleague ________________ *(smoke)* in the office. I ________________ *(hate)* it.
e The children ________________ *(watch)* too much TV.
f My wife ________________ *(go)* to the sauna every Tuesday.

4. Übersetzen Sie das Verb ins Englische und setzen Sie es in die richtige Form.

a Henry ________________ *(studiert)* the Wall Street trends on the internet.
b Helen ________________ *(versucht)* to keep fit.
c She ________________ *(tut)* her best to keep fit.
d I ________________ *(beende)* work at 3 on Friday.
e We ________________ *(mögen)* France.
f The Smiths ________________ *(haben)* a holiday apartment in St. Tropez.

2 I don't smoke.

Ich rauche nicht.

I / You don't smoke – Tim doesn't smoke

Diese Formen mit don't und doesn't sind etwas gewöhnungsbedürftig, denn wörtlich heißen sie „ich tue nicht rauchen", „du tust nicht rauchen", „Tim tut nicht rauchen". Die Verneinung mit don't / doesn't ist aber kein Stolperstein mehr, wenn man sie einmal richtig geübt hat.

Regel Wir verneinen die einfache Gegenwart, indem wir do + not (Kurzform: don't) oder does + not (Kurzform: doesn't) vor das Verb setzen.

I you we they	**don't smoke**

he she it	**doesn't smoke**

! Nicht: ~~I smoke not. He smokes not.~~

We **don't work** on Sundays. *Wir arbeiten sonntags nicht.*
They **don't like** fish. *Sie mögen keinen Fisch.*
I **don't play** football. *Ich spiele nicht Fußball.*
Helen **doesn't like** beer. *Helen mag kein Bier.*
He **doesn't drive**. *Er fährt nicht Auto.*

Nach doesn't entfällt die -s-Endung des Verbs.
My partner **works** part-time. He **doesn't work** (nicht: doesn't ~~works~~) full-time.
Mein Partner arbeitet Teilzeit. Er arbeitet nicht Vollzeit.

1. Kreuzen Sie die richtige Form an.

a My colleagues … .
- don't smoke
- doesn't smoke

b David … French.
- don't speak
- doesn't speak

c I … fish.
- don't eat
- eat not

d Angela … coffee.
- doesn't drink
- doesn't drinks

e This bus … to the station.
- doesn't go
- goes not

f The banks … on Sundays.
- don't open
- doesn't open

2. Bilden Sie verneinte Sätze wie im Beispiel.

I drink coffee. *(tea)* I don't drink tea.

a We go out at the weekend. *(in the week)* ________________

b My husband speaks Italian. *(Spanish)* ________________

c It costs $40. *($50)* ________________

d Mary lives alone. *(with her boyfriend)* ________________

e They open six days a week. *(on Sundays)* ________________

f I have enough time. *(enough money)* ________________

3. Ergänzen Sie die richtige Form des Verbs.

a I ________________ *(not drink)* when I ________________ *(drive)*. It's too risky.

b My son ________________ *(say)* that he ________________ *(not want)* to go to university.

c Our neighbours both ________________ *(work)*, so we ________________ *(not see)* them much. We ________________ *(not know)* many people here yet.

d They ________________ *(not take)* credit cards, and I ________________ *(not think)* I have enough cash. Can you help?

e The 7.43 is a fast train and ________________ *(not stop)* in Wendover.

f The brochure ________________ *(not say)* how much it ________________ *(cost)* without breakfast.

4. Übersetzen Sie das Verb ins Englische und setzen Sie es in die richtige Form.

a Mary ________________ *(wohnt)* in Paris but she ________________ *(spricht nicht)* much French.

b My sister ________________ *(hat)* two children. She ________________ *(arbeitet nicht)*.

c My friend ________________ *(spielt nicht)* tennis, but she ________________ *(schaut)* it on TV.

d Normally I ________________ *(arbeite nicht)* at weekends.

e Our children ________________ *(wollen nicht)* to go on holiday with us.

f I ________________ *(schreibe)* e-mails, but I ________________ *(surfe nicht)* much.

3 She never buys magazines.

Sie kauft nie Zeitschriften.

[1] Ich wette

she never buys – she always reads

never und always sind Häufigkeitsangaben. Wo stehen sie in Bezug zum Verb? Diese Unit beschäftigt sich mit der – vom Deutschen abweichenden – Wortstellung.

Regel always (immer), usually (meistens), normally (normalerweise), often (oft), sometimes (manchmal) und never (nie) stehen vor dem Verb und seinen Ergänzungen.

		Verb + Ergänzung(en)	
Tim	**always**	reads the paper.	*Tim liest immer die Zeitung.*
Tina	**usually**	drinks tea.	*Tina trinkt meistens Tee.*
We	**often**	meet friends in town.	*Wir treffen oft Freunde in der Stadt.*
I	**sometimes**	walk to work.	*Ich gehe manchmal zu Fuß zur Arbeit.*
Sue	**never**	drinks alcohol.	*Sue trinkt nie Alkohol.*

Auch in verneinten Sätzen steht die Häufigkeitsangabe vor dem Verb – in diesem Fall hinter don't / doesn't

We	don't	**always**	eat breakfast.	*Wir frühstücken nicht immer.*
Tina	doesn't	**usually**	drink coffee.	*Tina trinkt meistens keinen Kaffee.*

Angaben mit every (jede/r/s) stehen jedoch am Satzende.

Tim reads the paper **every morning**.	*Tim liest jeden Morgen die Zeitung.*
We don't have a hot meal **every day**.	*Wir essen nicht jeden Tag warm.*

! Häufigkeitsangaben stehen nicht – wie im Deutschen – zwischen Verb und Ergänzung(en).
Tim liest immer die Zeitung. ~~Tim reads always the paper.~~

1. Kreuzen Sie die richtige Form an.

a The train … on time.
- ☐ never arrives
- ☐ arrives never

b She … .
- ☐ swims every morning 500m
- ☐ swims 500m every morning

c We … TV in bed.
- ☐ sometimes watch
- ☐ watch sometimes

d I don't … .
- ☐ wash every day my hair
- ☐ wash my hair every day

e They … by car.
- ☐ don't always come
- ☐ don't come always

f You … .
- ☐ help never
- ☐ never help

2. Setzen Sie die Angabe in Klammern an der richtigen Stelle ein.

a She smiles at me. *(always)* ____________

b We don't go to the sauna. *(every week)* ____________

c They don't phone us before they come. *(always)* ____________

d I cook for friends on Sunday. *(often)* ____________

e It snows a lot here. *(never)* ____________

f They don't have a holiday. *(every year)* ____________

3. Bilden Sie Sätze.

always / I / eat / in the canteen *I always eat in the canteen.*

a never / I / very fast / drive ____________

b he / a glass of red wine / every day / drinks ____________

c don't / we / a paper / always / buy ____________

d me / my daughter / sometimes / helps ____________

e start / the car / doesn't / first time / always ____________

f washes / every Saturday / Dave / his car ____________

4. Übersetzen Sie.

a Wir gehen nie am Wochenende schwimmen.

b Ich stehe immer sehr früh auf.

c Mein Sohn hört *(listen to)* jeden Abend laute Musik.

d Ich übernachte *(stay)* nicht oft in Hotels.

e Meine Kollegin geht oft ins Kino.

f Mittags *(For lunch)* essen wir meistens Salat.

What does this mean?
Was bedeutet das?

What does this mean?

Tim fragt ganz korrekt What does this mean? (nicht: ~~What means this?~~) Wörtlich heißt seine Frage: „Was tut dies bedeuten?“ – hier geht es um die Fragebildung mit do und does.

Regel Fragen in der einfachen Gegenwart bilden wir mit dem Hilfsverb do. Wir setzen do (bei I, you, we, they) oder does (bei he, she, it) hinter dem Fragewort ein.

I have some cash.	How much	**do** I have?	*Wie viel habe ich?*
You work part-time.	When	**do** you work?	*Wann arbeitest du?*
We know something.	What	**do** we know?	*Was wissen wir?*
They live in America.	Where	**do** they live?	*Wo wohnen sie?*
He smokes.	Why	**does** he smoke?	*Warum raucht er?*
Ann likes music.	What kind	**does** she like?	*Welche Art (von Musik) mag sie?*
She jogs.	How often	**does** she jog?	*Wie oft joggt sie?*
It costs a lot.	How much	**does** it cost?	*Wie viel kostet es?*

Nach does entfällt die -s-Endung des Verbs.
He smokes. Why **does** he smoke (nicht: does he smoke~~s~~)?

do kann in einer Frage zweimal vorkommen – als Hilfsverb und Vollverb.
What **do** you **do**? *Was machen Sie beruflich?*
When **do** you **do** your homework? *Wann machen Sie Ihre Hausaufgaben?*
What kind of sports **do** you **do**? *Was für Sportarten machen Sie?*
He works every weekend. – Why **does** he **do** that? *Warum macht er das?*

1. Ergänzen Sie do oder does.

a When ________________ the film start?
b How ________________ I find out her name?
c Where ________________ you write the address?
d How much ________________ it cost?
e What ________________ this word mean?
f How often ________________ you meet?
g Why ________________ he never say hello?
h Where ________________ she play tennis?

2. Bilden Sie Fragen mit … do you … .

How *do you keep* fit? *(keep)* – I jog and I do aerobics.
a Where ______________________________? *(live)* – Not far from the airport.
b What ______________________________? *(do)* – I'm a technician.
c Where ______________________________ on holiday? *(go)* – Usually to Ireland.
d How ______________________________? *(travel)* – I fly.
e How long ______________________________? *(stay)* – Two weeks usually.
f What ______________________________ there? *(do)* – I go fishing.

3. Ergänzen Sie Fragen mit What kind of … („Was für …").

Ann likes music. *What kind of music does she like?*
a David drives a foreign car. ______________________________
b My neighbours have a dog. ______________________________
c I write books. ______________________________
d We like exotic food. ______________________________
e Tony plays an instrument. ______________________________
f I need a card for Anita. ______________________________

4. Übersetzen Sie.

a Was bedeutet dieses Wort?
b Wie oft trainieren Sie?
c Wo wohnen Ihre Eltern?
d Wann stehen Sie auf?
e Wo arbeitet Ihr Sohn?

5 Do you like it?

Gefällt es dir?

Do you …? – Yes, I do.

Der Einsatz von do in Fragen ist Ihnen aus Unit 4 bekannt. Hier geht es um eine weitere Eigenart des Englischen, nämlich die Kurzantwort (hier: Yes, I do), in der das Hilfsverb wiederholt wird.

Regel Fragen, auf die man mit „ja“ oder „nein“ antwortet (so genannte Entscheidungsfragen), bildet man in der einfachen Gegenwart mit dem Hilfsverb do. Die Frage beginnt mit Do oder Does. Auf solche Fragen antwortet man mit einer Kurzantwort, in der das Hilfsverb (do oder does – verneint: don't oder doesn't) wiederholt wird. Ein „nacktes“ yes oder no als Antwort wirkt oft unhöflich.

Do I	have time?	Yes, I **do**. / No, I **don't**.
Do you		Yes, you **do**. / No, you **don't**.
Do we		Yes, we **do**. / No, we **don't**.
Do they		Yes, they **do**. / No, they **don't**.
Does he	start at 7?	Yes, he **does**. / No, he **doesn't**.
Does she		Yes, she **does**. / No, she **doesn't**.
Does it		Yes, it **does**. / No, it **doesn't**.

Do you speak English? – Yes, I **do**. *Sprechen Sie Englisch? – Ja.*
Do his parents know? – No, they **don't**. *Wissen es seine Eltern? – Nein.*
Does your daughter like Sydney? – Yes, she **does**. *Mag Ihre Tochter Sydney? – Ja.*
Does the reservation cost extra? – No, it **doesn't**. *Kostet die Reservierung extra? – Nein.*

Nach does entfällt die -s-Endung des Verbs.
He **smokes**. – **Does** he **smoke** (nicht: smokes) cigars? *Er raucht. – Raucht er Zigarren?*

1. Ergänzen Sie do, don't, does oder doesn't.

a ______________ you need help? – Yes, I ______________ .
b ______________ the train stop in Risborough? – No, it ______________ .
c ______________ your friends speak Spanish? – No, they ______________ .
d ______________ Tony do any sport? – No, he ______________ .
e ______________ the boss know? – Yes, she ______________ .
f ______________ Ann eat meat? – No, she ______________ .

2. Beantworten Sie die Fragen für sich mit Yes, I do oder No, I don't.

a Do you like fish? – ______________
b Do you speak French? – ______________
c Do you play an instrument? – ______________
d Do you live in a flat? – ______________
e Do you listen to the radio much? – ______________
f Do you travel a lot? – ______________

Nehmen Sie ein Blatt und schreiben Sie die Fragen mit Does he / she … um, sodass sie sich auf Ihren besten Freund / Ihre beste Freundin beziehen. Schreiben Sie und beantworten Sie die Fragen.
Beispiel: *Does he/she like fish? – No, he/she doesn't.*

3. Ergänzen Sie die Fragen.

Does he play an instrument? *(play)* – Yes, he does, the guitar.
a ______________ *(eat)* a big lunch? – No, our main meal is in the evening.
b ______________ *(get up)* early? – Yes, we do. At 5.45.
c ______________ *(know)* his phone number? – Yes, she does. It's 427931.
d ______________ *(work)* very hard? – Yes, but she likes her job.
e ______________ *(cost)* much? – Yes, it does. $130.
f ______________ *(do)* much sport? – No, I'm a real couch potato.

4. Übersetzen Sie die Fragen und die Antworten.

a Wohnen Sie hier? – Ja.
b Kennt Tom die Adresse? – Ja.
c Mag sie Rosen? – Ja.
d Spielen sie Tennis? – Nein.
e Spricht der Präsident Deutsch? – Nein.

6 We're installing our new computer.

Wir installieren unseren neuen Computer.

we're ...ing

Diese Verbform kennen wir im Deutschen nicht: die Verlaufsform der Gegenwart (Englisch: *present continuous* oder *present progressive*). Sie beschreibt Handlungen und Vorgänge, die gerade jetzt im Verlauf begriffen sind.

[1]Plug & play = Reinstecken und sofort spielbereit.

Regel Die Verlaufsform der Gegenwart bildet man mit einer Form von be (am, is oder are) + Verb mit der Endung -ing.
Die Verneinung mit not kann man (außer bei I) auf zweierlei Weise bilden.

I'm	(= I am)	eating.
He's	(= He is)	
She's	(= She is)	
It's	(= It is)	
You're	(= You are)	
We're	(= We are)	
They're	(= They are)	

I'm not		working.
He's not	/ He isn't	
She's not	/ She isn't	
It's not	/ It isn't	
You're not	/ You aren't	
We're not	/ We aren't	
They're not	/ They aren't	

I'm listening to the radio. *Ich höre (gerade) Radio.*
Glenn isn't watching a video. *Glenn schaut (gerade) kein Video an.*
Let's wait. It's raining. *Lasst uns warten. Es regnet (gerade).*
The boys are playing football. *Die Jungs spielen (gerade) Fußball.*

Stummes -e entfällt vor -ing.

come – coming *kommen*
give – giving *geben*
have – having *haben, nehmen*
leave – leaving *weggehen, verlassen*
make – making *machen*
smoke – smoking *rauchen*
take – taking *nehmen*
write – writing *schreiben*

Der Endkonsonant wird bei manchen Verben vor -ing verdoppelt.

get – getting *besorgen, werden, kriegen*
plan – planning *planen*
put – putting *setzen, stellen, legen*
shut – shutting *schließen*
sit – sitting *sitzen*
stop – stopping *aufhören, stoppen*
swim – swimming *schwimmen*
travel – travelling *reisen*

1. Ergänzen Sie das Verb in der Verlaufsform.

a Just a moment. I ________________________ *(finish)* my breakfast.
b The neighbours ________________________ *(have)* a party and the music is very loud.
c Sonia's not here. She ________________________ *(play)* squash with a friend.
d I ________________________ *(write)* this letter on a train.
e Tom ________________________ *(sit)* at the computer in the next room.
f We ________________________ *(wait)* for Phil. He's late.
g Ann's in the bathroom. She ________________________ *(have)* a shower.
h The phone ________________________ *(ring)*. Can you answer it, please?

2. Ergänzen Sie wie im Beispiel.

a
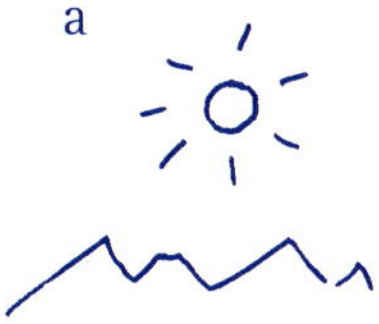
b

c

d

a It *isn't raining*. *(not rain)* The sun *is shining*. *(shine)*
b Tony ________________________ today. *(not work)*
He ________________________ tennis. *(play)*
c We ________________________ this evening. *(not cook)*
We ________________________ out. *(eat)*
d I ________________________ TV. *(not watch)*
I ________________________ my homework! *(do)*
e You ________________________. *(not listen)*
You ________________________ out of the window! *(look)*
f The children ________________________. *(not play)*
They ________________________ at the table. *(sit)*

e

f

3. Bilden Sie passende Sätze (teilweise verneinte Sätze) zum Bild.

(work) *He isn't working.*
a *(relax at home)*
b *(sit in a chair)*
c *(watch TV)*
d *(listen to music)*
e *(talk on the telephone)*
f *(use a mobile phone)*

7 He's just painting the kitchen.

Er streicht gerade die Küche.

he's just ...ing

Die Verlaufsform der Gegenwart gebraucht man oft mit Zeitangaben wie just (gerade), now (jetzt), at the moment (im Augenblick), today (heute), this week / month / year (diese Woche / diesen Monat / dieses Jahr). In dieser Unit geht es um die – vom Deutschen abweichende – Stellung solcher Zeitbestimmungen.

Regel

just / now
at the moment / today
this week / month / year

Vergangenheit	Gegenwart	Zukunft

just, now, at the moment, today, this week / month / year bezeichnen den jetzigen Zeitpunkt bzw. den aktuellen Zeitraum und sind Signalwörter für den Gebrauch der Verlaufsform der Gegenwart.

just steht vor der -ing-Form, sonst stehen diese Zeitbestimmungen am Satzende (manchmal auch am Satzanfang).

She is **just** leaving the office. *Sie verlässt gerade das Büro.*

He is packing the car **now**. *Er packt jetzt das Auto.*

We are watching an old film **at the moment**. *Wir sehen im Augenblick einen alten Film.*

I'm not working **today**. *Ich arbeite heute nicht.*

We aren't doing anything special **this evening**. *Wir machen heute Abend nichts Besonderes.*

! Zeitbestimmungen der Gegenwart können nicht – wie im Deutschen – zwischen Verb und Ergänzung(en) stehen.

Sie verlässt gerade das Büro. ~~She is leaving just the office.~~

Die Verlaufsform der Gegenwart (2)

7

Signalwörter *just, now* usw.

1. Die durchgestrichene Zeitangabe steht falsch. Korrigieren Sie den Satz.

a I am finishing ~~just~~ my supper. ____________________

b The sun isn't ~~today~~ shining. ____________________

c She's having ~~at the moment~~ a shower. ____________________

d The children are watching ~~just~~ a video. ____________________

e He's reading ~~now~~ your fax. ____________________

f We aren't going ~~this year~~ on holiday. ____________________

2. Bilden Sie einen Satz mit just wie im Beispiel.

a

leave

b

bring

c

tell

d

make

e

switch

f

take off

a Sorry, too late. The taxi *is just leaving.*

b They ____________________ our new sofa.

c Daniel ____________________ the boss the news.

d I ____________________ some tea. Would you like some?

e One moment, please. She ____________________ the computer off.

f The plane ____________________.

3. Bilden Sie Sätze und setzen Sie das Verb in die Verlaufsform.

a to work / this week / Tina / walk ____________________

b eat / at the moment / We / a lot of salads ____________________

c I / not use / now / the computer ____________________

d do / at the moment / My husband / a lot of sport ____________________

e try out / a new producer in China / We / at the moment ____________________

____

f to the Hanover Fair / this year / We / not go ____________________

4. Übersetzen Sie. Verwenden Sie immer die Verlaufsform.

a Es fängt gerade an zu regnen.

b Wir bleiben heute Abend zu Hause.

c Meine Frau arbeitet im Moment sehr hart.

d Ich warte jetzt auf seine Antwort.

e Jemand gebraucht *(use)* im Augenblick den Kopierer *(copier).*

f Wir besprechen *(discuss)* das Projekt heute Nachmittag.

8 Is it raining?

Regnet es?

Is it ...ing? – No, it isn't.

Fragen und Kurzantworten in der einfachen Gegenwart waren Thema in den Units 4 und 5. Jetzt geht es um die Bildung solcher Satztypen in der Verlaufsform.

Regel Fragen, auf die man mit „ja" oder „nein" antwortet (so genannte Entscheidungsfragen), bildet man in der Verlaufsform durch Umstellung von Subjekt (= die Person, die etwas tut) und Hilfsverb (am, are, is). Die -ing-Form bleibt unverändert.

Auf solche Fragen antwortet man mit einer Kurzantwort, in der das Hilfsverb (am, are oder is) wiederholt wird. Ein „nacktes" yes oder no als Antwort wirkt oft unhöflich.

I am	working.	Am I	working?	Yes, I am.	/ No, I'm not.
He is		Is he		Yes, he is.	/ No, he isn't.
She is		Is she		Yes, she is.	/ No, she isn't.
We are		Are we		Yes, we are.	/ No, we aren't.
You are		Are you		Yes, you are.	/ No, you aren't.
They are		Are they		Yes, they are.	/ No, they aren't.

Fragen mit Fragewörtern wie what, where, why bildet man auf die gleiche Weise. Das Fragewort steht am Satzanfang.

What is he doing? *Was macht er da gerade?*

Where are you staying? *Wo wohnen Sie?*

How are your parents travelling this time? *Wie reisen Ihre Eltern diesmal?*

Where is she sitting? *Wo sitzt sie?*

Why are we stopping? *Warum halten wir an?*

1. Ergänzen Sie am, are oder is.

a __________ Ann coming with us?
b What __________ that man doing?
c Where __________ all these people going?
d Why __________ I doing this?
e __________ Tom's friends helping him?
f __________ your son studying English?

2. Beantworten Sie die Fragen mit Yes, I am oder No, I'm not.

a Are you working at home? __________
b Are you sitting at a desk? __________
c Are you listening to music? __________
d Are you using a pen? __________
e Are you learning something? __________
f Are you feeling good? __________

3. Ergänzen Sie die Fragen zu dem Bild auf S. 24 und beantworten Sie sie.

(Tina / wear) Is Tina wearing jeans? – Yes, she is.
a *(she / wear)* __________ a pullover? – __________
b *(Tim / wear)* __________ jeans? – __________
c *(he / carry)* __________ a bag? – __________
d *(Tina / ask)* __________ him a question? – __________
e *(Tim and Tina / go)* __________ to work? – __________
f *(Tim / feel)* __________ happy? – __________

4. Übersetzen Sie die Fragen und Kurzantworten. Verwenden Sie die Verlaufsform.

a Warum lachen Sie?
b Was studiert Ihre Tochter?
c Kommt Anja [mit][1]? – Ja.
d Schauen die Kinder [gerade][1] fern? – Ja.
e Arbeitet deine Frau heute? – Nein.
f Was sagt er [da gerade][1]?

[1] Wörter in eckigen Klammern müssen nicht übersetzt werden.

9 He's watching Wimbledon. He watches it every year.

Er schaut Wimbledon an. Er schaut es jedes Jahr an.

now ... every year

he <u>is watching</u> [now] heißt es, aber he <u>watches</u> every year: In dieser Unit geht es um den unterschiedlichen Gebrauch von Verlaufsform und einfacher Form der Gegenwart.

Regel

Mit der **einfachen Gegenwart** sagen wir, was immer (always, every day/week/month/year), meistens (usually, normally), oft (often), manchmal (sometimes) oder auch nie (never) geschieht.
Mit der einfachen Gegenwart beschreiben wir Gewohnheiten und andere regelmäßige Geschehen.

Tim **usually cooks.**

It **always rains** a lot here.
Es regnet hier immer viel.
Ann **plays** tennis **every** Tuesday.
Ann spielt jeden Dienstag Tennis.
Tom **usually gets up** late on Sunday.
Tom steht am Sonntag meistens spät auf.
I **don't often watch** sport on TV.
Ich schaue nicht oft Sport im Fernsehen.
We **sometimes eat** out on Fridays.
Wir gehen manchmal freitags essen.
I **never work** on Sundays.
Ich arbeite sonntags nie.
What **do** you **do** on Friday evenings?
Was macht ihr freitags abends?

Mit der **Verlaufsform der Gegenwart** sagen wir, was gerade (just), jetzt (now), im Augenblick (at the moment), heute (today), diese Woche/diesen Monat/dieses Jahr (this week/month/year) geschieht.
Mit der Verlaufsform beschreiben wir einen Vorgang, der gerade im Verlauf begriffen ist.

I **am cooking today.**

But **now** it's **snowing.**
Aber jetzt schneit es (gerade).
Today she **is playing** in a tournament.
Heute spielt sie in einem Turnier.
It's 11 o'clock now and he's **just getting up.**
Es ist jetzt 11 Uhr und er steht gerade auf.
But I'**m just watching** some tennis.
Aber ich schaue gerade [etwas] Tennis.
But **today** we **are eating** at home.
Aber heute essen wir zu Hause.
But my wife **is working this weekend.**
Aber meine Frau arbeitet dieses Wochenende.
What **are** you **doing at the moment?**
Was macht ihr im Moment?

1. Kreuzen Sie die richtige Form an.

a We ... our neighbours.
- ☐ are never seeing
- ☐ never see

b I ... to the news.
- ☐ am just listening
- ☐ just listen

c Dave ... at the weekend.
- ☐ is usually phoning
- ☐ usually phones

d How many people ... now?
- ☐ are waiting
- ☐ wait

e It ... at the moment.
- ☐ doesn't rain
- ☐ isn't raining

f This ... .
- ☐ doesn't often happen
- ☐ isn't often happening

2. Ergänzen Sie die Sätze zum Bild auf S. 26.

a Tim and Tina normally ________________ *(watch)* only one TV of course.
b But Tim ________________ *(watch)* two at the same time today.
c Tina ________________ *(talk)* to a friend at the moment.
d Tim ________________ *(just watch)* the end of an exciting match.
e Tim never ________________ *(play)* tennis.
f He never ________________ *(do)* much sport, but he often ________________ *(watch)* it.

3. Bilden Sie verneinte Sätze mit don't / doesn't (einfache Gegenwart) oder aren't / isn't (Verlaufsform).

The train doesn't usually stop *(not usually stop)* here.
It isn't raining *(not rain)* at the moment.

a We ______________________________ *(not do)* anything special at the moment.
b I ______________________________ *(not normally smoke)*, but I sometimes have a cigar.
c The neighbours ______________________________ *(not make)* much noise this evening.
d Customers ______________________________ *(not normally pay)* in cash.
e My boss has a new baby, so she ______________________________ *(not work)* at the moment.
f I ______________________________ *(not usually arrive)* home before 7 in the evening.

4. Bilden Sie Fragen mit einer Form von do (einfache Gegenwart) oder von be (Verlaufsform).

Do you always put *(you / always / put)* sugar in the salad? – Sometimes, but not often.
Is Ann using *(Ann / use)* the computer at the moment? – No, it's free now.

a ______________________________ *(Phil / work)* this weekend? – Yes, today, but not tomorrow.
b How often ______________________________ *(you / go)* away at the weekend? – Once a month.
c ______________________________ *(you / often / visit)* your parents? – No, not often.
d ______________________________ *(your boss / travel)* a lot at the moment? – Yes. At the moment he's in Rome.
e When ______________________________ *(you / usually start)* work? – At 8.30.
f What ______________________________ *(you / do)* at the moment? – I'm making supper.

10 I'm fasting for five days.
Ich faste fünf Tage.

[1]Flüssigkeit

I'm only drinking.

Tim trinkt gerade nicht und trotzdem gebraucht er die Verlaufsform I'm only drinking. Warum? Weil er eine vorübergehende Situation beschreibt. In dieser Unit beschäftigen wir uns mit weiteren Besonderheiten der Verlaufsform.

Regel

Mit der **einfachen Gegenwart** sagen wir, was regelmäßig in bestimmten Abständen geschieht.
Wir beschreiben damit einen Dauerzustand.

We **live** in a two-room flat.
Wir wohnen in einer Zweizimmerwohnung.
My husband **works** for Siemens.
Mein Mann arbeitet bei Siemens.
He **drives** to work.
Er fährt mit dem Auto zur Arbeit.
This company **buys** components from Asia.
Diese Firma kauft Bauteile aus Asien ein.

Mit der **Verlaufsform der Gegenwart** sagen wir, was jetzt gerade im Augenblick geschieht. Wir beschreiben damit auch vorübergehende Situationen von begrenzter Dauer, die gerade aktuell sind.

Our guests **are staying** in a hotel.
Unsere Gäste wohnen im Hotel.
He **is working** at home this week.
Er arbeitet diese Woche zu Hause.
But this week he **is going** by bus.
Aber diese Woche fährt er mit dem Bus.
We **are testing** a new supplier in Taiwan.
Wir testen einen neuen Lieferanten in Taiwan.

Mit der Verlaufsform beschreiben wir auch Entwicklungen und Veränderungen, die jetzt im Gange sind und noch nicht abgeschlossen sind. Dazu zählen auch längere Lern- und Ausbildungssituationen.

The company **is expanding** fast. *Die Firma expandiert [zurzeit] schnell.*
Our climate **is changing**. *Unser Klima verändert sich.*
I **am learning** Italian. I **am doing** an intensive course.
Ich lerne Italienisch. Ich mache einen Intensivkurs.
Ann **is studying** law. Peter **is training** to be a media designer.
Ann studiert Jura. Peter macht eine Ausbildung als Mediendesigner.

1. Beschreiben Sie die Veränderungen mit einem Satz in der Verlaufsform.

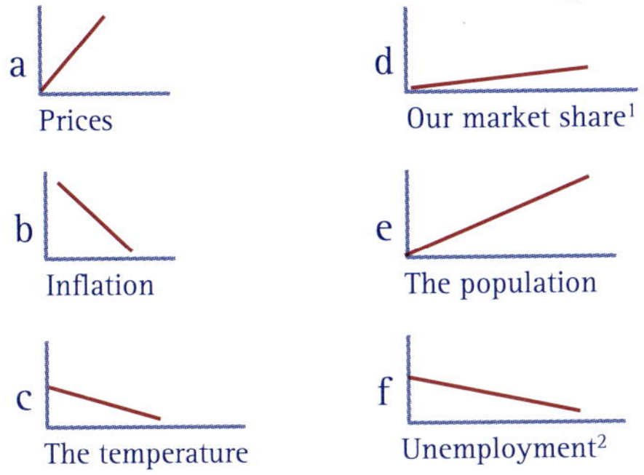

a *(rise)* Prices are rising.
b *(fall)* ____________
c *(drop)* ____________
d *(increase)* ____________
e *(grow)* ____________
f *(go down)* ____________

[1]Marktanteil [2]Die Arbeitslosigkeit

2. Entscheiden Sie: Ist normalerweise ein Dauerzustand (D) oder eine vorübergehende Situation (V) gemeint?

Und nun ergänzen Sie mit den Verben links.

D	V			
☐	✔	a	build a house	They are building a new house on that field by the church.
☐	☐	b	live in a house	My friends ____________ in a house with a big garden.
☐	☐	c	stay in a house *(as a guest)*	My mother-in-law ____________ with us for 3 weeks.
☐	☐	d	study medicine	Tina's son is very clever. He ____________ medicine.
☐	☐	e	teach English *(as a job)*	Tina ____________ English at a girls' school.
☐	☐	f	make progress[1]	My mother is in hospital, but she ____________ progress.

[1]Fortschritte

3. Ergänzen Sie die Verben: eat, learn, paint, shine, speak, work, work.

a It's a lovely day and the sun *(scheint)* ____________.
b We *(streichen)* ____________ our flat. It's a lot of work.
c I *(lerne)* ____________ Italian. Tom *(spricht)* ____________ it very well.
d The weather is very hot so we *(essen)* ____________ a lot of cold food.
e Angela *(arbeitet)* ____________ for an American company in London. This week she *(arbeitet)* ____________ at the company's office in Berlin.

4. Bilden Sie Fragen mit einer Form von do (einfache Gegenwart) oder be (Verlaufsform).

a What ____________ *(you / do)*? ____________ *(you / wait)* for somebody? – Yes, my daughter. She's late.
b Which newspaper ____________ *(you / read)*? – The *Times* in the week, and the *Observer* on Sunday.
c Where ____________ *(you / go)*? – To the supermarket for some milk.
d How ____________ *(you / get)* to work? – By car usually.
e ____________ *(you / speak)* French? – No, sorry.

11

I need a drink.

Ich brauche einen Drink.

I need ... now

I need a drink now – ein ganz aktueller, im Moment bestehender Wunsch von Tina und trotzdem wählt sie die einfache Form und nicht die Verlaufsform des Verbs. In dieser Unit geht es um die kleine Gruppe von Verben, die nicht in der Verlaufsform gebraucht werden.

Regel Eine kleine Gruppe von Verben, die nicht eine Tätigkeit, sondern einen Zustand bezeichnen, wird nur in der einfachen Form verwendet.

like *mögen, gern haben/tun*	want *wollen*	mean *bedeuten*
love *lieben, sehr gern haben/tun*	believe *glauben*	seem *(er)scheinen*
hate *hassen, ungern haben/tun*	remember *sich erinnern*	depend on *abhängen von*
prefer *lieber haben/tun*	forget *vergessen*	belong to *gehören*
need *brauchen*	understand *verstehen*	know *wissen, kennen*

Ben **likes** France, but I **prefer** Italy. *Ben mag Frankreich, aber ich mag Italien lieber.*
I **believe** you now. I **know** you're right. *Ich glaube dir jetzt. Ich weiß, dass du Recht hast.*
Do you **remember** that paella? *Erinnerst du dich an diese Paella?*
The castle **belongs to** a film star now. *Das Schloss gehört jetzt einem Filmstar.*

Je nach Bedeutung können have und think in der Verlaufsform stehen oder auch nicht.
They **have** a horse now. *Sie haben [= besitzen] jetzt ein Pferd.*
Sorry, I **have** no time today. *Leider habe ich heute keine Zeit [zur Verfügung].*
Dave **is having** a shower. *Dave duscht [= nimmt eine Dusche].*
Ann **is having** salad / coffee today. *Ann isst heute Salat / trinkt heute Kaffee.*
We **are having** a lovely holiday. *Wir haben [= erleben gerade] einen wunderbaren Urlaub.*
We **are having** a great time. *Wir amüsieren uns großartig.*
I **think** it's too expensive. What **do** you **think**? *Ich meine, es ist zu teuer. Was meinst du?*
We **are thinking of** going to France again. *Wir überlegen wieder nach Frankreich zu fahren.*
I'm **thinking about** your problem. *Ich denke über dein Problem nach.*

1. Ergänzen Sie das Verb in der einfachen Form.

a Tony ________________ *(think)* it's a good idea now.
b Can you go to the supermarket? We ________________ *(need)* some bread and milk.
c Ann ________________ *(not want)* it now, so shall I throw it away?
d We ________________ *(not understand)* how it could happen.
e I ________________ *(not remember)* the price. $80? $90? ________________ *(you / remember)*?

2. Übersetzen Sie. Verwenden Sie die einfache Form.

a I ________________ *(will)* to buy a new mobile phone, but I ________________ *(weiß nicht)* which one to buy. It all ________________ *(hängt ab von)* the price.
b We ________________ *(mögen nicht)* it here. We ________________ *(kennen nicht)* many people.
c ________________ *(Verstehen Sie)* what he's saying? I ________________ *(verstehe nicht)* much.
d The Ford ________________ *(gehört)* my neighbour, but I ________________ *(weiß nicht)* who drives the white Toyota.

3. Ergänzen Sie die einfache Form oder Verlaufsform von have.

a In their postcard they say that they ________________ a great holiday.
b It's OK, I ________________ enough money for us both.
c How many children ________________ the Smiths ________________?
d It's Tony's 30th birthday, and he ________________ a big party.
e What sort of car ________________ you ________________?
f Sorry, he ________________ a bath. Can you phone back later?

4. Ergänzen Sie die einfache Form oder Verlaufsform von think.

a What's the time? – I ________________ it's about six o'clock.
b I ________________ we should go. We don't want to be late.
c They ________________ of moving out of the city to a place in the mountains.
d Don't go in now. She ________________ about that computer problem.
e I ________________ Phil knows the answer. Ask him.
f ________________ you ________________ it's a good idea? I ________________ it's great.

5. Ergänzen Sie die Verben in der passenden Form.

a I ________________ *(wait)* for a phone call from my boss. I ________________ *(want)* to know if he ________________ *(have)* time to see me today.
b We ________________ *(think)* of buying a new car. I ________________ *(think)* a diesel is best.
c Sorry, she ________________ *(have)* lunch at the moment. She always ________________ *(have)* lunch between 12 and 1.
d Anything else? – No thanks. At the moment I ________________ *(have)* all that I ________________ *(need)*.
e What ________________ you ________________ *(think)*? Is it a good idea? – It ________________ *(seem)* so.

Units 1–11

Wählen Sie die richtige Form.

Einfache Form und Verlaufsform der Gegenwart

1. My brother ... to America every month.
   a) flies
   b) fly

2. Sally usually ... work at 6 o'clock.
   a) finishes
   b) finishs

3. I ... and drive.
   a) drink not
   b) don't drink

4. My partner ... on Thursday or Friday.
   a) doesn't work
   b) doesn't works

5. I ... tea in the morning.
   a) drink usually
   b) usually drink

6. Tony .... It's so unfair.
   a) helps never
   b) never helps

7. What ...?
   a) does 'daffodil' mean
   b) means 'daffodil'

8. Why ... to work? It's so near, she could walk.
   a) does Ann drive
   b) does Ann drives

9. Do you need more time? – ...
   a) Yes, I do.
   b) Yes, I need.

10. Does your colleague know about these plans? – ...
    a) No, he doesn't.
    b) No, he not.

11. Where's Ann? – She ... over there under the tree.
    a) is lieing
    b) is lying

12. Tony ... his e-mails.
    a) is checking just
    b) is just checking

13. I think Philip is having ....
    a) at the moment his supper
    b) his supper at the moment.

14. Are you waiting for someone? – ...
    a) Yes, I am.
    b) Yes, I'm.

15. What ... here?
    a) are all those people doing
    b) are doing all those people

16. Ann ... every Tuesday evening.
    a) goes swimming
    b) is going swimming

17. I ... time to watch TV.
    a) don't often have
    b) 'm not often having

18. Can you help me for a moment? What ...?
    a) are you doing
    b) do you do

19. We could go for a walk now if you like. It … .
    a) ☐ doesn't rain
    b) ☐ isn't raining

20. We … to Italy for our holidays.
    a) ☐ are often going
    b) ☐ often go

21. Four of our guests … here. The rest are in the Oxford Hotel.
    a) ☐ are staying
    b) ☐ stay

22. E-commerce … as fast as people thought.
    a) ☐ doesn't grow
    b) ☐ isn't growing

23. I … at home this week. I have a project that I want to finish.
    a) ☐ am working
    b) ☐ work

24. My partner … Italian. The teacher is a lady from Rome.
    a) ☐ is learning
    b) ☐ learns

25. The winters here must be hard. … to work in the winter, too? – Yes, all year round.
    a) ☐ Are you driving
    b) ☐ Do you drive

26. At the moment prices … again.
    a) ☐ are falling
    b) ☐ fall

27. It's very expensive. What …? Should we buy it?
    a) ☐ are you thinking
    b) ☐ do you think

28. I … about selling the car, but I don't know if now is a good time.
    a) ☐ am thinking
    b) ☐ think

29. What … now? I'm working. Can't you see?
    a) ☐ are you wanting
    b) ☐ do you want

30. They've bought a new house. They … a swimming pool now.
    a) ☐ are having
    b) ☐ have

Vergleichen Sie nun Ihre Lösungen mit dem Schlüssel auf S. 152. Wenn Sie Aufgaben nicht richtig gelöst haben, wiederholen Sie noch einmal die betreffende Unit. Diese Tabelle zeigt Ihnen, auf welche Unit sich die einzelnen Aufgaben beziehen.

Aufgabe	Unit	Aufgabe	Unit
1	1	16	9
2	1	17	9
3	2	18	9
4	2	19	9
5	3	20	9
6	3	21	10
7	4	22	10
8	4	23	10
9	5	24	10
10	5	25	10
11	6	26	10
12	7	27	11
13	7	28	11
14	8	29	11
15	8	30	11

12 I was here first.

Ich war zuerst da.

I was, you weren't, it was

Der Cartoontext enthält gleich drei Beispiele der Vergangenheitsform (Englisch: *simple past*) des Verbs be. Diese Zeitstufe macht keine großen Probleme, denn es gibt nur zwei Formen, was und were.

Regel Die Vergangenheit von am und is heißt was, die Vergangenheit von are heißt were. Die Verneinung ist wasn't (= was not) oder weren't (= were not).

I / he / she / it	**was / wasn't**
we / you / they	**were / weren't**

I **was** with friends last night. *Ich war gestern Abend mit Freunden zusammen.*
Ben **was** ill yesterday. He **wasn't** at work. *Ben war gestern krank. Er war nicht in der Arbeit.*
We **weren't** here last week. *Wir waren letzte Woche nicht hier.*
You **were** here before me. *Du warst vor mir da.*

Fragen beginnen mit Was / Were bzw. Fragewort + was / were. Was / Were wird in der Kurzantwort wiederholt.

Was I / he / she / it here?	Yes, I / … **was.**	No, I / … **wasn't.**
Were we / you / they here?	Yes, we / … **were.**	No, we / … **weren't.**

Was the film good last night? – No, it **wasn't.** It was awful. *War der Film gestern Abend gut? – Nein. Er war schrecklich.*
Were your parents strict? – No, they **weren't.** Not very. *Waren deine Eltern streng? – Nein. Nicht sehr.*
What **was** the weather like? *Wie war das Wetter?*
Where **were** [!] you born? *Wo sind Sie geboren?*
Where **were** you yesterday? *Wo warst du gestern?*

1. Kreuzen Sie die richtige Form an.

a I … ill yesterday.
- ☐ was
- ☐ were

b The train … late every day last week.
- ☐ was
- ☐ were

c … you at Angela's party last weekend?
- ☐ Was
- ☐ Were

d It was Sunday so the shops … open.
- ☐ wasn't
- ☐ weren't

e You … very happy last weekend. Why?
- ☐ wasn't
- ☐ weren't

f The waiting room … very full.
- ☐ wasn't
- ☐ weren't

2. Ergänzen Sie was, wasn't, were oder weren't.

a Where is Ann? She ________________ here a moment ago.

b As a child I ________________ a great comic fan. Tom & Jerry ________________ my favourite characters.

c The hotel ________________ expensive. The room ________________ only $30 per night.

d Normally we're a group of ten, but four people ________________ there last Tuesday, so we ________________ only a small group of six.

e It ________________ 10 o'clock at night, so it ________________ easy to see the house because it ________________ dark.

f Dave and Ed ________________ on holiday in Rome last week. That's why they ________________ at the party.

3. Ergänzen Sie die Fragen mit was / were und beantworten Sie sie für sich.

Were you a happy child when you *were* young? – *Yes, I was. / No, I wasn't.*

a ________________ you tall for your age *(Alter)*? – ________________, I ________________.

b ________________ your house/flat big? – ________________, it ________________.

c ________________ your first day at school a shock? – ______________________________

d ________________ the school far from your house/flat? – ______________________________

e ________________ most of your teachers nice? – ______________________________

f ________________ you good at sports? – ______________________________

4. Übersetzen Sie.

a Wo warst du gestern? Warst du krank?

b Wie war euer Urlaub? – Er war toll.

c Das Wetter und das Hotel waren beide sehr gut.

d Die Reise war sehr lang. Sie war nicht leicht *(easy)*.

e Die Eltern waren nicht zu Hause. Die Kinder waren allein.

f Wann war Angelo hier? War es letztes Jahr?

13 It worked yesterday.
Gestern funktionierte er.

it worked yesterday

It worked yesterday entspricht „Gestern funktionierte er“ bzw. „Gestern hat er funktioniert“. Wenn man von der Vergangenheit spricht, kann man im Deutschen oft beliebig zwischen zwei Formen („funktionierte“ oder „hat funktioniert“) wählen. Im Englischen ist dies nicht möglich. Näheres hierzu in den Units 16 und 20–22.

Regel Wir bilden die Vergangenheitsform regelmäßiger Verben, indem wir -ed an die Grundform anhängen. Diese Form ist für alle Personen gleich, auch für he, she und it.
Die Verneinung bilden wir, indem wir didn't (= did not) vor die Grundform stellen. Auch didn't ist für alle Personen gleich.

GEGENWART:	I watch films, but I don't watch sport. *Ich sehe Filme, aber ich sehe keinen Sport.*
VERGANGENHEIT:	I watch**ed** *Casablanca* yesterday, but I **didn't** watch the football. *Ich habe gestern* Casablanca *gesehen, aber ich habe nicht Fußball gesehen.*
GEGENWART:	Tim works on Saturdays, but he doesn't work on Sundays. *Tim arbeitet samstags, aber er arbeitet sonntags nicht.*
VERGANGENHEIT:	Tim work**ed** last Saturday, but he **didn't** work on Sunday. *Tim hat letzten Samstag gearbeitet, aber er hat am Sonntag nicht gearbeitet.*

! Nach didn't steht die Grundform des Verbs, die -ed-Endung entfällt.
I watch**ed** TV yesterday, but I **didn't** watch (~~didn't watched~~) breakfast TV.

! Die Verneinung von was / were wird nicht mit didn't gebildet (→ Unit 12).
I **wasn't** (~~didn't be~~) at work yesterday. We **weren't** (~~didn't be~~) back from our holiday.
Ich war gestern nicht in der Arbeit. Wir waren noch nicht aus dem Urlaub zurück.

Stummes -e entfällt vor -ed:
arrive – arrived *ankommen* live – lived *wohnen* phone – phoned *telefonieren*

Nach einem Konsonanten wird -y + -ed zu -ied:
hurry – hurried *eilen* study – studied *studieren* try – tried *versuchen*

Der Endkonsonant wird bei manchen Verben vor -ed verdoppelt:
plan – planned *planen* stop – stopped *aufhören* travel – travelled *reisen*

1. Kreuzen Sie die richtige Form an.

a I … very long at the meeting.
- ☐ didn't stay
- ☐ stayed not

b We … to phone you.
- ☐ tried
- ☐ tryed

c They … it all a long time ago.
- ☐ planed
- ☐ planned

d It … much.
- ☐ didn't rain
- ☐ didn't rained

e The accident … last week.
- ☐ did happen
- ☐ happened

f We … late.
- ☐ arriveed
- ☐ arrived

2. Setzen Sie die Verben in die Vergangenheitsform.

a We ______________ *(live)* there over 20 years.
b A mobile phone ______________ *(start)* to ring in the middle of the concert.
c The train suddenly ______________ *(stop)*.
d My mother ______________ *(study)* physics.
e An old school friend ______________ *(phone)* me last night.

3. Bilden Sie verneinte Sätze wie im Beispiel.

I asked David. *(Peter)* I didn't ask Peter.
a We played tennis. *(mini-golf)* ______________
b They cleaned the floor. *(windows)* ______________
c Angela planned the conference. *(conference party)* ______________
d I ordered beer. *(wine)* ______________
e We arrived separately. *(together)* ______________

4. Ergänzen Sie die Vergangenheitsform des Verbs.

a They ______________ *(want)* to stay longer, but they ______________ *(not like)* the hotel.
b I ______________ *(enjoy)* the holiday. I ______________ *(not miss)* the office for one moment!
c We ______________ *(plan)* to go to Rome, but then we ______________ *(visit)* Florence instead.
d It ______________ *(start)* to rain so I ______________ *(hurry)* home.
e It all ______________ *(seem)* so easy – but it ______________ *(not be)*!

5. Übersetzen Sie die Verben. Verwenden Sie immer die Vergangenheitsform.

a We ______________ *(haben gesehen)* a late-night film on TV and we ______________ *(sind nicht gegangen)* to bed before 2 o'clock.
b I ______________ *(habe gefragt)* because it ______________ *(schien)* important.
c We ______________ *(lernten nicht)* much. We ______________ *(spielten)* all the time.
d I ______________ *(habe es nicht geplant)* like this – it just ______________ *(passierte)*!
e I ______________ *(habe versucht)* to talk to him, but he ______________ *(wollte nicht)* to know.

14 It fell out of my hands.

Sie fiel mir aus den Händen.

fell, didn't fall

fell ist die Vergangenheitsform des unregelmäßigen Verbs fall. Solche Formen muss man wohl oder übel auswendig lernen. Bei der Verneinung ist es leichter; sie setzt sich – wie bei regelmäßigen Verben – aus didn't + Grundform zusammen.

Regel Wir bilden die Vergangenheitsform unregelmäßiger Verben nicht mit -ed, sondern sie haben besondere Formen. Die wichtigsten sind hier aufgelistet. Weitere siehe Anhang, S. 166.

break	**broke**	*(zer)brechen, kaputt gehen*
buy	**bought**	*kaufen*
come	**came**	*kommen*
cost	**cost**	*kosten*
do	**did**	*tun, machen*
drink	**drank**	*trinken*
drive	**drove**	*(Auto) fahren*
eat	**ate**	*essen*
fall	**fell**	*fallen*
feel	**felt**	*(sich) fühlen*
find	**found**	*finden*
fly	**flew**	*fliegen*
forget	**forgot**	*vergessen*

get	**got**	*bekommen, besorgen*
give	**gave**	*geben*
go	**went**	*gehen, fahren*
have	**had**	*haben*
hear	**heard**	*hören*
know	**knew**	*wissen, kennen*
leave	**left**	*verlassen; weggehen/fahren*
lose	**lost**	*verlieren*
make	**made**	*machen*
meet	**met**	*(sich) treffen*
pay	**paid**	*bezahlen*

put	**put**	*stellen, legen*
read	**read**	*lesen*
ring	**rang**	*anrufen*
say	**said**	*sagen*
see	**saw**	*sehen*
sit	**sat**	*sitzen*
speak	**spoke**	*sprechen*
take	**took**	*nehmen*
tell	**told**	*erzählen*
think	**thought**	*denken; meinen*
understand	**understood**	*verstehen*
write	**wrote**	*schreiben*

We **flew** to Italy and **went** to Venice.

Wir sind nach Italien geflogen und nach Venedig gefahren.

I **found** a new boutique and **bought** some new things.

Ich entdeckte eine neue Boutique und kaufte einige neue Sachen.

Wie bei regelmäßigen Verben bilden wir die Verneinung mit didn't.

We **didn't meet** (~~didn't met~~) yesterday. Donna **didn't have** (~~didn't had~~) time.

Wir haben uns gestern nicht getroffen. Donna hatte keine Zeit.

Auch die Vergangenheit von do wird mit didn't gebildet.

Tanja **did** all the work, but she **didn't do** it alone.

Tanja hat die ganze Arbeit gemacht, aber sie hat sie nicht allein gemacht.

Vergangenheitsform (3)

Unregelmäßige Verben

1. Kreuzen Sie die richtige Form an.

a We ... to Paris last weekend.
- ☐ flied
- ☐ flew

b We ... in a café.
- ☐ sat
- ☐ sitted

c I ... great.
- ☐ fall
- ☐ felt

d I ... to the waiter in English.
- ☐ speaked
- ☐ spoke

e He ... me.
- ☐ didn't understand
- ☐ didn't understood

f We ... much sightseeing.
- ☐ didn't
- ☐ didn't do

2. Ergänzen Sie die richtige Vergangenheitsform.

a My father once ________________ *(find)* 50,000 Italian lire in the street. He ________________ *(take)* it to the police station, but they ________________ *(not want)* it. They ________________ *(give)* it back to him.

b We ________________ *(not know)* many of the other guests at the party last week, but we ________________ *(have)* a good time. I ________________ *(speak)* to a lot of interesting people. We ________________ *(eat)* some fantastic food, and they ________________ *(have)* some lovely wine. But I ________________ *(not drink)* any because I had to drive.

c This time we ________________ *(not pay)* so much. It ________________ *(cost)* less than last year.

d We ________________ *(not do)* much at the weekend. The weather ________________ *(not be)* very good, so we ________________ *(stay)* at home, ________________ *(read)*, ________________ *(listen)* to music and ________________ *(watch)* one or two videos. I even ________________ *(write)* a letter.

e Yesterday some friends ________________ *(come)* round. We last ________________ *(meet)* a long time ago, so we ________________ *(have)* a lot to tell each other.

f Sorry, I ________________ *(forget)* to tell you about the meeting when I ________________ *(see)* you last week. Then Dave ________________ *(tell)* me not to phone. He ________________ *(say)* that you ________________ *(know)*.

3. Übersetzen Sie die Verben. Verwenden Sie immer die Vergangenheitsform.

a I hear that you ________________ *(hast verloren)* your mobile phone yesterday. – Yes, somebody ________________ *(hat genommen)* it from my bag.

b Last week Sandra's mother ________________ *(ist gefallen)* and ________________ *(hat gebrochen)* her leg.

c Somebody ________________ *(hat gestellt)* a vase of flowers on my desk yesterday. Was it you, Angela? – No, I ________________ *(habe nicht getan)* it.

d We ________________ *(hörten)* from an old friend last week. We last ________________ *(haben gesehen)* him in 2001.

e She ________________ *(kaufte)* an ice-cream, then ________________ *(saß)* in the park.

Did you know?
Hast du das gewusst?

Did you ...?

Aus den Units 4–5 ist Ihnen die Fragebildung mit do bekannt (z. B. Do you know? = „Wissen Sie es?“) und aus den Units 13–14 did als Vergangenheitsform von do. Sicher erkennen Sie nun, warum es in Tinas Frage Did you know heißt (und nicht ~~Knew you~~).

Regel Fragen nach der Gegenwart bilden wir mit do und does. Fragen nach der Vergangenheit bilden wir mit did. did ist die Vergangenheitsform von sowohl do als auch does.

GEGENWART:	**Do** you work at weekends? *Arbeitest du an Wochenenden?*
	Does Tim work at weekends? *Arbeitet Tim an Wochenenden?*
VERGANGENHEIT:	**Did** you work last weekend? *Hast du letztes Wochenende gearbeitet?*
	Did Tim work last weekend? *Hat Tim letztes Wochenende gearbeitet?*

did wird in der Kurzantwort wiederholt.

	I		Yes, I **did**.	No, I **didn't**.
Did	he / she / it	go?	Yes, he / she / it **did**.	No, he / she / it **didn't**.
	we / you / they		Yes, we / you / they **did**.	No, we / you / they **didn't**.

Fragen mit einem Fragewort bilden wir ebenfalls mit did.
When **did** you arrive? (~~When arrived you?~~) *Wann sind Sie angekommen?*
What **did** the boss say? (~~What said the boss?~~) *Was hat der Chef gesagt?*

Auch wenn wir fragen, was jemand getan hat, kommt did zum Einsatz. In diesen Fragen heißt es did ... do.
What **did** you do yesterday? (~~What did you yesterday?~~) *Was hast du gestern gemacht?*
Why **did** he do this to me? (~~Why did he this to me?~~) *Warum hat er mir das angetan?*
Did the dog do this? (~~Did the dog this?~~) *Hat der Hund das hier gemacht?*

1. Ergänzen Sie did und didn't.

a ______________ I tell you that story about Tim? – No, you ______________.
b ______________ you find out the address? – Yes, I ______________.
c ______________ they phone back? – No, they ______________.
d ______________ the man pay cash? – Yes, he ______________.
e ______________ the waitress understand your French? – No, she ______________.
f ______________ the teacher know? – Yes, she ______________.

2. Bilden Sie Fragen mit ... did you ... .

Where _did you buy_ *(buy)* that dress? – In Spain.
a When ______________________ *(arrive)* home? – Very late. After midnight.
b Where ______________________ *(park)*? – In Castle Street.
c How ______________________ *(find out)* about this? – On the internet.
d Who ______________________ *(see)*? – Lots of people. It was a really great party.
e A broken leg? How ______________________ *(do)* that? – I fell off my bike.
f What ______________________ *(do)* last night? – I stayed at home and watched TV.

3. Ergänzen Sie die Fragen und beantworten Sie sie für sich mit Yes, I did oder No, I didn't.

Did you go *(go)* to the cinema last week? – _Yes, I did. / No, I didn't._
a ______________________ *(sleep)* well last night? – ______________________
b ______________________ *(get up)* early this morning? – ______________________
c ______________________ *(watch)* TV last night? – ______________________
d ______________________ *(go out)* last weekend? – ______________________
e ______________________ *(stay)* at home last Christmas? – ______________________
f ______________________ *(buy)* a newspaper yesterday? – ______________________

4. Vervollständigen Sie die Übersetzungen. Verwenden Sie did.

a Hat es gestern geregnet?
______________________________ yesterday?
b Wie ist es passiert?
______________________________ happen?
c Wie haben seine Eltern es herausgefunden?
______________________________ find out?
d Hatten Sie eine gute Reise?
______________________________ journey?
e Wie viel hat es gekostet?
How much ______________________________?

16 When did you buy this?

Wann hast du das gekauft?

When did you . . .?

Auf Deutsch hieße Tinas Frage wohl „Wann hast du das hier gekauft?" – mit einer Perfektform („hast . . . gekauft"). Im Englischen steht jedoch nach when? die englische Vergangenheitsform (did . . . buy). In dieser Unit geht es um Zeitangaben, die den Gebrauch der englischen Vergangenheitsform zwingend erfordern.

Regel Bei Zeitangaben, die einen festen Zeitpunkt oder Zeitraum der abgeschlossenen Vergangenheit bezeichnen, müssen wir die englische Vergangenheitsform verwenden:

- when? (wann?), yesterday (gestern)
- Ausdrücke mit last: last night, last week, last Monday, last month, last May, last year
- Ausdrücke mit Uhrzeiten und Wochentagen: at 6 o'clock, on Monday [= letzten Montag]
- Ausdrücke mit Monaten, Daten und Jahreszahlen: in June, on 18th June, in 2001
- Ausdrücke mit ago: two weeks ago (vor zwei Wochen), an hour ago (vor einer Stunde)

When did you **move** here? *Wann seid ihr hierher gezogen?*
I saw Jane **yesterday**. *Ich habe gestern Jane gesehen.*
We **went** to the theatre **last week**. *Wir sind letzte Woche ins Theater gegangen.*
We **didn't go** out **on Sunday**. *Am Sonntag sind wir nicht ausgegangen.*
I **flew** to Chile **in April 2001**. *Im April 2001 bin ich nach Chile geflogen.*
Tom **sent** me an e-mail **three days ago**. *Tom hat mir vor drei Tagen eine E-Mail geschickt.*

! ago entspricht „vor" und steht am Ende einer Zeitbestimmung, nicht am Anfang.
vor zwei Tagen = two days **ago** (~~for two days~~) vor einer Stunde = an hour **ago** (~~for an hour~~)

! Diese Zeitbestimmungen stellen wir an den Satzanfang oder ans Satzende. Sie können nicht – wie im Deutschen – zwischen Verb und Ergänzungen stehen.
Yesterday I saw Jane. oder: I saw Jane **yesterday**. (~~I saw yesterday Jane.~~)
Last week I bought a car. oder: I bought a car **last week**. (~~I bought last week a car.~~)

1. Ergänzen Sie das Verb in der Vergangenheitsform.

a This letter ________________ *(arrive)* yesterday.
b My team ________________ *(lose)* last weekend.
c Tony ________________ *(leave)* two hours ago.
d It ________________ *(happen)* in September 2001.
e We ______________________ *(not meet)* on Sunday.
f It ______________________ *(not snow)* in January.
g When ____________________________ *(you tell)* Philip?
h When ____________________________ *(this e-mail arrive)*?

2. Machen Sie wahre Aussagen über sich.

Beispiel: I ________________ *(work)* last weekend.
I worked last weekend. *oder:* I *didn't work* last weekend.

a I ______________________ *(watch)* TV yesterday.
b I ______________________ *(travel)* by train last week.
c I ______________________ *(start)* to learn English two years ago.
d I ______________________ *(have)* breakfast at 6.30 this morning.
e I ______________________ *(live)* here in 1999.

3. Bilden Sie Sätze. Achten Sie auf die Verbform und die Satzstellung.

(live / here / I / in 1999) *I lived here in 1999.*

a *(fish / I / yesterday / eat)* ____
b *(Ann / on 6th June / a big party / give)* ______________________________________
c *(We / time / on Friday / not have)* ____
d *(so much / The taxi / last time / not cost)* ____________________________________
e *(They / in 2002 / a holiday / not have)* _______________________________________
f *(The postman / bring / ten minutes ago / these two letters)* ______________________
____

4. Übersetzen Sie.

a vor fünf Tagen ______________________
b vor einer Stunde ______________________
c vor drei Jahren ______________________
d vor einem Monat ______________________
e vor zehn Minuten ______________________
f vor zwei Wochen ______________________

5. Übersetzen Sie. Verwenden Sie die englische Vergangenheitsform.

a Wann sind Sie angekommen?
b Wir haben das Haus vor vier Jahren gekauft.
c Herr Smith ist vor zwei Tagen gestorben.
d Ann und Ian haben 2001 geheiratet.
e Ich habe diesen Film letztes Jahr im Kino gesehen.

17

I was watching the football.

Ich schaute gerade Fußball.

I was ...ing

Die Verlaufsform der Gegenwart (z. B. I <u>am</u> watching TV) ist Ihnen aus den Units 6–8 bekannt. Jetzt kommt die Verlaufsform der Vergangenheit dazu (I <u>was</u> watching TV). Bildung und Anwendung sind bei beiden Verlaufsformen ähnlich.

Regel Die Verlaufsform der Vergangenheit (Englisch: *past continuous* oder *past progressive*) bilden wir mit was / were + Verb mit der Endung -ing.

		Verneinung			Frage	
I / He / She / It	was working.	I / He / She / It	was not (wasn't)	playing.	Was I / Was he / Was she / Was it	working?
We / You / They	were working.	We / You / They	were not (weren't)	playing.	Were we / Were you / Were they	working?

Mit der Verlaufsform der Vergangenheit beschreiben wir einen Vorgang, der zu einem bestimmten Zeitpunkt gerade im Verlauf begriffen war.

It's 6.30 now. Tony **is having** breakfast.
Es ist jetzt 6.30 Uhr. Tony frühstückt gerade.
At 6.00 he **was having** a shower.
Um 6.00 Uhr hat er (gerade) geduscht.

It **was raining** hard at lunchtime, so I stayed in the office.
Mittags regnete es (gerade) stark, also bin ich im Büro geblieben.
People **were standing** in the street. They **were waiting** for the film star.
Menschen standen (gerade) auf der Straße. Sie warteten (gerade) auf den Filmstar.
Who **was driving** at the time – you or your husband?
Wer fuhr zu der Zeit – Sie oder Ihr Mann?

1. Ergänzen Sie das Verb in der Verlaufsform der Vergangenheit.

a I saw Lynn today. She ________________ *(talk)* to a friend.
b Angela looked fantastic. She ________________ *(wear)* a long black dress.
c It was fantastic. People ________________ *(dance)* in the streets.
d It was lunchtime, so parents ________________ *(wait)* outside school for their children.
e It was a warm evening and we ________________ *(sit)* in the garden.
f You ________________ *(smoke)*. I saw you.

2. Widersprechen Sie wie im Beispiel.

You were smoking. – I *wasn't smoking*. I *was chewing* *(chew)* bubblegum!
a It was raining. – It ________________. The sun ________________ *(shine)*!
b Dave was cooking. – He ________________. He ________________ *(wash up)*.
c You were surfing. – I ________________. I ________________ *(write)* an e-mail!
d The pupils were working hard. – They ________________ hard. They ________________ *(talk)*.
e Ann was buying something. – She ________________ anything. She ________________ *(just look)*.
f We were playing cards. – We ________________ cards. We ________________ *(watch)* football!

3. Ergänzen Sie die Fragen und Antworten in der Verlaufsform der Vergangenheit.

What *were you doing* *(you / do)*? – I *was going* *(go)* to my evening class.
a Why ________________________ *(they / laugh)*? – Because Tina ______________ *(tell)* jokes.
b Where ________________________ *(you / live)* at the time? – In Washington. Sonia ________________ *(work)* for an advertising agency there.
c What ________________________ *(you / do)* in Castle Street this morning? – I ________________ *(try)* to find somewhere to park!
d Why ________________________ *(she / wear)* that dress? – She ________________ *(go)* to a wedding.
e ________________________ *(you / wait)* for someone? – Yes, I ________________ *(wait)* for a friend.
f ________________________ *(David / drive)*? – No, he ________________ *(sit)* in the back with the children.

4. Übersetzen Sie ins Englische. Die Verben stehen in der Verlaufsform.

a It was a beautiful day. *Die Vögel sangen und die Sonne schien.*
b A policeman was already there. *Er interviewte den Inhaber* (owner) *des Ladens.*
c I thought of you this morning. *Was hast du um 8 Uhr gemacht?*
d It was 12 minutes past 3 when we got to the station. *Der Zug fuhr gerade los* (leave).
e The train was awfully full. *Menschen standen in den Gängen* (gangways). *Einige saßen auf dem Boden.*
f We weren't expecting vistors. *Wir trugen unsere ältesten Sachen. Wir arbeiteten im Garten.*

I was filling it when the phone rang.

Ich füllte sie gerade, als das Telefon klingelte.

was . . .ing when . . .
Tims Erklärung der Überschwemmung enthält zwei Verben. Das erste steht in der Verlaufsform der Vergangenheit (was filling), das andere in der einfachen Form (rang). In dieser Unit geht es um den unterschiedlichen Gebrauch dieser beiden Formen.

Regel Mit der Verlaufsform der Vergangenheit beschreiben wir eine „Hintergrundsituation“, die von einem anderen Geschehen unterbrochen wurde. Die Unterbrechung steht in der Vergangenheitsform.

I was **playing** a computer game when my boss **walked** in. *Ich spielte gerade ein Computerspiel, als mein Chef hereinkam.*

We **were having** lunch when Ann **arrived.** *Wir aßen gerade zu Mittag, als Ann kam.*

Die Verlaufsform beschreibt eine Tätigkeit, die zu einem bestimmten Zeitpunkt noch im Verlauf begriffen war.

I was **filling** the watering can
when the phone rang.
Ich füllte gerade die Gießkanne,
als das Telefon klingelte.
Ben **was washing** the car
when it started to rain.
Ben war dabei, das Auto zu waschen,
als es anfing zu regnen.
At 8 o'clock I **was having** breakfast.
I **was reading** the paper.
Um 8 Uhr frühstückte ich (gerade).
Ich las (gerade) die Zeitung.

Die einfache Form beschreibt eine fertig abgeschlossene Tätigkeit, oft in einer Kette von hintereinander ablaufenden Handlungen.

I **filled** the watering can,
then **watered** the flowers.
Ich habe die Gießkanne gefüllt,
dann habe ich die Blumen gegossen.
Ben **washed** the car,
then **drove** it into the garage.
Ben hat das Auto gewaschen,
dann hat er es in die Garage gefahren.
I **had** breakfast,
then at 8.15 I **left** the house.
Ich habe gefrühstückt,
dann verließ ich um 8.15 Uhr das Haus.

1. Kreuzen Sie die richtige Form an.

a

c

b

d

a I ☐ had / ☐ was having a bath when the phone ☐ rang / ☐ was ringing.
b Mary ☐ saw / ☐ was seeing an accident when she ☐ drove / ☐ was driving to work yesterday morning.
c When Bill ☐ went / ☐ was going outside, lots of people ☐ waited / ☐ were waiting at the taxi stand.
d We ☐ had / ☐ were having dinner in the restaurant when Dave ☐ came / ☐ was coming in.

2. Ergänzen Sie. Verwenden Sie die Verlaufsform der Vergangenheit für die Hintergrundsituation, die einfache Form für die Unterbrechung.

I *was watching* *(watch)* TV when Tina *arrived* *(arrive)* home.
a I ________________ *(have)* a shower when the guests ________________ *(arrive)*.
b We ________________ *(eat)* supper when all the lights suddenly ________________ *(go)* out.
c The bomb ________________ *(explode)* near a bus-stop where people ________________ *(wait)* for a bus.
d I ________________ *(discuss)* the new brochure with the sales manager when the designer ________________ *(phone)*.
e I ________________ *(wait)* for my plane when I ________________ *(see)* somebody that I knew.
f The postman ________________ *(come)* while we ________________ *(have)* breakfast.

3. Übersetzen Sie.

a Als wir ankamen, schien [schon][1] die Sonne.
b Sie aß [gerade][1] ein Sandwich, als ich ihr das Fax brachte.
c Ich putzte [gerade][1] meine Zähne, als der Briefträger kam.
d Ich nahm die Post und schloss *(lock)* die Tür ab.
e Ich las den Brief, als mein Chef hereinkam.
f Ich las den Brief und gab ihn meinem Chef.

[1]Wörter in eckigen Klammern müssen nicht übersetzt werden.

You've eaten all my chocolates.

Du hast meine ganzen Pralinen gegessen.

you have eaten

Diese Verbform nennen wir Present Perfect. Sie setzt sich zusammen aus dem Hilfsverb have und dem Verbteil (Partizip) eaten.
Die ähnliche Verbform im Deutschen *(hast gegessen)* heißt Perfekt. Diesen Namen verwenden wir jedoch bewusst nicht, weil die Verwendung von Present Perfect im Englischen und Perfekt im Deutschen erhebliche Unterschiede aufweist.

Regel Wir bilden das Present Perfect mit have / has + Partizip Perfekt.
Bei regelmäßigen Verben ist dieses Partizip identisch mit der Vergangenheitsform (→ Unit 13) und hat die Endung -ed.

I / You / We / They	**have started.**	I / You / We / They	**haven't (= have not) finished.**
He / She / It	**has started.**	He / She / It	**hasn't (= has not) finished.**

Bei unregelmäßigen Verben ist das Partizip zum Teil identisch mit der Vergangenheitsform, zum Teil aber nicht. (Vollständige Liste s. Anhang, S. 166)
buy – **bought** – **bought** We **have bought** a new car. *Wir haben ein neues Auto gekauft.*
drive – **drove** – **driven** We **have driven** 50 kilometres. *Wir sind 50 Kilometer gefahren.*

bring	brought	**brought**	*bringen*	hear	heard	**heard**	*hören*
buy	bought	**bought**	*kaufen*	know	knew	**known**	*kennen, wissen*
come	came	**come**	*kommen*	lose	lost	**lost**	*verlieren*
do	did	**done**	*tun, machen*	make	made	**made**	*machen*
drink	drank	**drunk**	*trinken*	meet	met	**met**	*treffen, begegnen*
drive	drove	**driven**	*fahren*	pay	paid	**paid**	*(be)zahlen*
eat	ate	**eaten**	*essen*	read	read	**read**	*lesen*
find	found	**found**	*finden*	say	said	**said**	*sagen*
fly	flew	**flown**	*fliegen*	see	saw	**seen**	*sehen*
forget	forgot	**forgotten**	*vergessen*	speak	spoke	**spoken**	*sprechen*
go	went	**gone**	*gehen*	take	took	**taken**	*nehmen*
have	had	**had**	*haben*	write	wrote	**written**	*schreiben*

1. Kreuzen Sie die richtige Form an.

a Oh no. It ... started to rain.
- ☐ has
- ☐ have

b Tony and Linda ... come. Why?
- ☐ hasn't
- ☐ haven't

c Tom ... gone to the cinema.
- ☐ has
- ☐ is

d I've ... this film before.
- ☐ seen
- ☐ saw

e I have ... all the exercises.
- ☐ did
- ☐ done

f They've ... the bill.
- ☐ paid
- ☐ payed

2. Ergänzen Sie das Present Perfect dieser regelmäßigen Verben.

a I ______________ *(accept)* their offer. The job starts in November.
b You ______________ *(not answer)* my question.
c We ______________ *(organize)* a big party for Ben's birthday.
d It's good to have you back. I ______________ *(miss)* you.
e Why are all the doors open? What ______________ *(happen)*?
f It ______________ *(not rain)* here. The weather is good.

3. Ergänzen Sie das Present Perfect dieser unregelmäßigen Verben.

a We can't get in. Ian ______________ *(lose)* the key.
b I ______________ *(make)* the coffee. We can have breakfast.
c It's Donna's birthday tomorrow. – I know, I ______________ *(not forget)*.
d I ______________ *(drink)* two glasses. Do you think I can still drive home?
e David ______________ *(bring)* a friend with him. Come and meet her.
f You're Ann's brother, aren't you? We ______________ *(meet)* before.

4. Übersetzen Sie. Verwenden Sie das Present Perfect.

a Ich habe mit *(to)* meinem Chef gesprochen.
b Die Kinder haben gelernt zu warten.
c Er hat die Rechnung *(bill)* nicht bezahlt.
d Angela hat eine neue Wohnung gefunden.
e Jemand hat unseren Parkplatz *(parking space)* genommen!

5. Schreiben Sie auf ein Blatt, was Sie heute gemacht und was Sie nicht gemacht haben.

do a lot of work / drink alcohol / drive a car / eat a hot meal / fly / hear/see a plane / make tea / meet a friend / read a paper / speak English / watch TV / write an e-mail

Beispiele: Das habe ich gemacht: *I've driven a car today.*

Das habe ich nicht gemacht: *I haven't drunk alcohol today.*

20 Have you ever thought about ...?

Hast du jemals darüber nachgedacht ...?

[1]ausgebrannte

Have you ever ...?

Tinas Frage mit ever ist ein typisches Beispiel für die Verwendung des Present Perfect. In dieser Unit lernen Sie, wann die Antwort im Present Perfect steht, wann in der Vergangenheitsform.

Regel Wenn wir danach fragen, ob jemand etwas jemals, schon einmal, in der ganzen Zeit bis jetzt getan hat, verwenden wir das Present Perfect mit ever.

Have you **ever eaten** seaweed? *Haben Sie jemals Seetang gegessen?*

Have you **ever driven** a sports car? *Haben Sie schon einmal einen Sportwagen gefahren?*

Have you **ever been** to Canada? *Waren Sie schon einmal in Kanada?*

Die Antwort kann eine Kurzantwort sein, in der das Hilfsverb have oder has wiederholt wird.

Have you ever flown? – Yes, I **have**. / No, I **haven't**. *Sind Sie je geflogen? – Ja. / Nein.*

Has he ever won? – Yes, he **has**. / No, he **hasn't**. *Hat er je gewonnen? – Ja. / Nein.*

Auch eine längere Antwort steht im Present Perfect, wenn die Zeitbestimmung never (nie, niemals) darin vorkommt.

Have you ever lost a lot of money? *Haben Sie jemals viel Geld verloren?*

– No, that **has never happened** to me. *Nein, das ist mir [noch] nie passiert.*

Oft jedoch beantworten wir eine Have you ever-Frage mit ja und geben dann weitere Einzelheiten, z. B. über Ort und Zeit. Eine solche längere Antwort steht in der Vergangenheitsform, wenn sie eine Zeitbestimmung wie yesterday, ago, last (week), in (2001), on (Monday), at (1 o'clock) enthält (→ Unit 16).

Have you ever lost a lot of money? – Yes, **two years ago I left** (~~have left~~) a jacket with €200 on a train. *Ja, vor zwei Jahren habe ich eine Jacke mit € 200 in einem Zug liegen lassen.*

Have you ever smoked? – Yes, but I **gave up** (~~have given up~~) **last year**. *Ja, aber ich habe letztes Jahr aufgehört.*

! Vor einem Orts- bzw. Ländernamen steht have / has been <u>to</u> und went <u>to</u>.

Have you ever **been to** (~~in~~) Portugal? *Waren Sie schon einmal in Portugal?*

I **went to** Lisbon last year. *Ich war letztes Jahr in Lissabon.*

1. Ergänzen Sie have, has, haven't oder hasn't.

a __________ you ever been to Scotland? – No, I __________.
b __________ Ben ever asked you for money? – No, he __________.
c __________ this train ever arrived on time? – Yes, of course it __________.
d __________ the Boltons ever invited you to a party? – No, they __________.
e __________ we ever done this before? – Yes, we __________. Of course.
f __________ you ever seen a fox here? – Yes, I __________. Often.

2. Ergänzen Sie die Fragen und beantworten Sie sie mit No, I have never ... oder mit Yes, I did that ... [+ Zeitpunkt].

Beispiel: Have you ever *stayed* *(stay)* in a five-star hotel?
No, I have never stayed in a five-star hotel.
oder: *Yes, I did that two years ago / in 2001 / last month / . . . .*

a Have you ever __________ *(be)* to Italy? __________
b Have you ever __________ *(try)* bungee-jumping? __________
c Have you ever __________ *(buy)* a cuckoo clock? __________
d Have you ever __________ *(speak)* to a politician[1]? __________
e Have you ever __________ *(fly)* to another continent? __________

[1]Politiker/in

3. Ergänzen Sie die Frage (immer Present Perfect) und die Antwort (immer Vergangenheitsform).

a __________ *(you / ever / be)* to Africa? – Yes, I __________ *(go)* to Egypt in 1999. I __________ *(see)* the pyramids. They __________ *(be)* great.
b __________ *(you / ever / buy)* something on the internet? – Yes, I __________ *(buy)* a new telephone last week. I __________ *(pay)* by credit card.
c __________ *(Tony / ever / see)* you in that outfit? – Of course. I __________ *(wear)* it last Saturday. We __________ *(be)* at a concert together.
d __________ *(we / ever / have)* snow in June? – Not here, but we __________ *(have)* some in Switzerland last year. Don't you remember? We __________ *(drive)* through some snow on the way home, too.
e __________ *(this team / ever / win)* an international match? – Of course. They __________ *(win)* against Ajax Amsterdam two years ago.

4. Übersetzen Sie.

a Waren Sie schon einmal in Australien?
b Letztes Wochenende sind wir nach Paris gefahren.
c Waren Sie schon einmal in den USA? – Ja. Ich bin 2002 *(in 2002)* in Florida gewesen.
d Ann war [schon einmal][1] in Kanada. Sie war vor zwei Jahren in Toronto.

[1]Wörter in eckigen Klammern müssen nicht übersetzt werden.

I have always wanted …

Ich wollte schon immer …

I've always wanted …

Tina wollte schon immer einen Pullover aus Lamawolle. Im Englischen heißt das: Tina has always wanted … . In dieser Unit geht es um Zeitbestimmungen, bei denen man im Englischen das Present Perfect verwendet.

Regel Bei Zeitbestimmungen, die einen festen Zeitpunkt oder Zeitraum der Vergangenheit bezeichnen, müssen wir im Englischen die Vergangenheitsform verwenden (→ Units 16, 20).
Das Present Perfect verwenden wir – neben ever und never (→ Unit 20) – bei folgenden Zeitbestimmungen[1]:

already *schon*	before *schon (ein)mal*	not yet *noch nicht*
yet? *schon?* [in Fragen]	lately / recently *in letzter Zeit*	so far *bisher, bis jetzt*
always *schon immer*	just *gerade*	

I've already **eaten**. *Ich habe schon gegessen.*
Has Peter **phoned** yet? *Hat Peter schon angerufen?*
I've always **wanted** a leather sofa. *Ich wollte schon immer ein Ledersofa.*
This **has happened** before. *Das ist schon mal passiert.*
Tony **has been** ill a lot recently / lately. *Tony war in letzter Zeit viel krank.*
I've just **had** lunch. *Ich habe gerade zu Mittag gegessen.*
The letter **hasn't arrived** yet. *Der Brief ist noch nicht angekommen.*
We've **collected** €200 so far. *Bisher / Bis jetzt haben wir € 200 gesammelt.*

!
1. Aussagesatz: *Tom ist schon angekommen.* = Tom has **already** arrived.
   Fragesatz: *Ist Tom schon angekommen?* = Has Tom arrived **yet**?
2. *Es hat in letzter Zeit viel geregnet.* = It has rained a lot **recently / lately**.

[1] Insbesondere im amerikanischen Englisch wird zum Teil die Vergangenheitsform benutzt. Gehen Sie jedoch besser auf Nummer Sicher und verwenden Sie das Present Perfect.

1. Übersetzen Sie die deutsche Zeitbestimmung.

a We haven't seen Claire much ________________ *(in letzter Zeit).*
b Have they paid ________________ *(schon)?* – No, they're late again.
c Hurry up! The first guests have ________________ *(schon)* arrived!
d I have eaten Indonesian food ________________ *(schon mal).*

2. Antworten Sie im Present Perfect mit der angegebenen Zeitbestimmung.

Can you tell the others, please? – I *have already told* them. *(already / tell)*
a Sorry I'm late. – It's OK. We ______________________________ *(not start / yet).*
b How much more time do you need? – I ______________________________ *(just / finish).*
c We can't go out in this rain. – It's OK. It ______________________________ *(just / stop).*
d Are you ready? – No, sorry. I ______________________________ *(not find my keys / yet).*
e Let's buy it. – We can't. We ______________________________ *(already / spend)* over $500.
f How's Ann? – I don't know. I ______________________________ *(not see her / lately).*

3. Übersetzen Sie die deutsche Zeitbestimmung und ergänzen Sie das Present Perfect.

It ________________ *(be* / schon immer) expensive to have good taste.
It *has always been* expensive to have good taste.
a Peter ________________ *(do)* this ________________ (schon mal). Many times.
b ______________________ *(you / tell)* your parents ________________ (schon)?
c Mrs Watson ____________________________ *(arrive* / schon). She's waiting in your office.
d We ________________ *(not have)* this problem very often ________________ (in letzter Zeit).
e I ________________ *(see)* this film ________________ (schon einmal).
f We ________________ *(have)* a lot of rain ________________ (in letzter Zeit).
g ______________________ *(Andy / finish)* his homework ________________ (schon)?

4. Present Perfect oder Vergangenheitsform? Verwenden Sie, wenn möglich, das Present Perfect.

Tipp: Unterstreichen Sie zuerst die Zeitbestimmungen. Danach erst ergänzen Sie.
I ______________________________ *(always / want)* to see the Grand Canyon.
I *have always wanted* to see the Grand Canyon.
We ______________________________ *(go)* to Peru last year.
We *went* to Peru last year.
a My brother ______________________________ *(go)* to Canada two years ago.
b I ______________________________ *(see)* this film in London last summer.
c Angela ______________________________ *(not come)* home yet.
d When ______________________________ *(this letter / arrive)*?
e This problem is new. This ______________________________ *(not happen)* before.
f Bill ____________________ *(start)* a diet last week. He ____________________ *(lose)* 3 kg so far.
g ______________________________ *(they / deliver)* the new fax machine yet?
When ______________________________ *(they / plan)* to bring it?

I've found them. They were ...

Ich habe sie gefunden. Sie waren ...

I've found ... they were ...

Unser Cartoon zeigt die Verwendung des Present Perfect (I've found) neben der Vergangenheitsform (They were). In diesem Fall ist der deutsche Sprachgebrauch genau parallel (Perfekt, dann Vergangenheitsform). Oft jedoch ist der Gebrauch dieser Zeitformen im Englischen und im Deutschen abweichend. Wann das der Fall ist, lernen Sie in dieser Unit.

Regel

Wenn wir sagen, dass jemand etwas irgendwann schon einmal, in der ganzen Zeit bis jetzt getan hat, verwenden wir das **Present Perfect.**

Wir sagen, dass etwas geschehen ist.
Wichtig ist das gegenwärtige Ergebnis.

I have read this book.
Ich habe dieses Buch gelesen.
[= Ich kenne es.]

Ann **has booked** a table.
Ann hat einen Tisch bestellt.
[= Ein Tisch ist reserviert.]

Wenn wir sagen, dass jemand etwas zu einem bestimmten vergangenen Zeitpunkt getan hat, verwenden wir die **Vergangenheitsform.**

Wir sagen, wann etwas geschehen ist.

I **read** an interesting article **last week.**
Ich habe letzte Woche einen interessanten Artikel gelesen.

We **booked** our summer holiday **yesterday.**
Wir haben gestern unseren Sommerurlaub gebucht.

Auch wenn der Zeitpunkt nicht explizit genannt, wohl aber gedacht wird, muss man im Englischen die Vergangenheitsform verwenden.

Susan Smith **has worked** in Japan.
Susan Smith hat in Japan gearbeitet.
[= Sie kennt die Gepflogenheiten dort.]

Mrs Johnson **has left.**
Mrs Johnson ist schon gegangen.
[= Heute ist sie nicht mehr zu sprechen.]

I've **paid** the bill.
Ich habe die Rechnung bezahlt.
[= Wir können jetzt gehen.]

My great-grandfather **worked** very hard.
Mein Urgroßvater arbeitete sehr hart.
[Damals, als er lebte.]

It was a long way, so we **left** home very early.
Wir sind sehr früh [um .. Uhr] aufgebrochen [als wir damals verreist sind].

We **paid** only DM 130,- for two nights.
Wir zahlten [damals] nur DM 130,- für zwei Nächte.

1. Ergänzen Sie das Present Perfect.

a I _______________ *(be)* to Toronto. It's a great city.
b Ann _______________ *(buy)* the wine. We've got everything for the party now.
c They _______________ *(have)* enough time. They must be ready now.
d Everything is quieter now because the school holidays _______________ *(finish)*.
e We _______________ *(have)* a lot of snow, so we're going skiing this weekend.
f Sally _______________ *(eat)* and says she doesn't want anything.

2. Ergänzen Sie in jedem Satz das angegebene Verb einmal im Present Perfect und einmal in der Vergangenheitsform. Beachten Sie die Zeitbestimmungen.

a The Smiths _______________; they _______________ to London two months ago. *(move)*
b The price _______________ up; it _______________ up last week. *(go)*
c All my friends _______________ the film, and I _______________ it last weekend. *(see)*
d I _______________n't _______________ Dave yet, but I _______________ Alan yesterday. *(tell)*
e We _______________ 600 last week, so we _______________ over 2000 altogether so far. *(sell)*
f The rain _______________; it _______________ five minutes ago. *(stop)*

3. Ist das kursiv (= schräg) Gedruckte richtig oder falsch? Wenn falsch, berichtigen Sie.

a I *have been* to New Zealand last year. _______________
b We are going to Sweden. I *wasn't* there before. _______________
c The weather *has been* very good *lately*. _______________
d My boss *has flown* to Houston on Saturday. He's back tomorrow. _______________
____
e I *always lived* here. All my life. _______________
f I have been to Canada. But I *was never in* the USA. _______________

4. Übersetzen Sie.

Tipp: Fragen Sie sich: Wird das jetzige Ergebnis berichtet *(= Present Perfect)* oder die vergangene Handlung (= Vergangenheitsform)?

a The hospital _______________ *(hat angerufen)* five minutes ago. Toby _______________ *(hatte)* a car accident and is badly hurt.
b Mr Swinson _______________ *(hat gearbeitet)* for Siemens before he _______________ *(ist gekommen)* here in September 2000.
c The documents _______________ *(sind gekommen)*. A courier _______________ *(hat gebracht)* them at 11 o'clock.
d I _______________ *(habe gepackt)* the children's things last night, but I _______________ *(habe nicht gepackt)* my things yet.
e Our neighbours _______________ *(sind gewesen in)* Australia three times. The last time they _______________ *(sind geflogen)* with Quantas, via Bangkok.

23 I've been here since 7.

Ich bin seit 7 hier.

Tina *Where are you?*
Tim *At the cinema. I've been here since 7. Where are you?*
Tina *At the cinema.*
Tim *You can't be.*
Tina *I am. I've been here for 20 minutes, too.*

I've been here since / for …

In dieser Unit geht es um wichtige Unterschiede zwischen dem englischen und deutschen Sprachgebrauch.

Tims Satz I've been here since 7 entspricht „Ich bin seit 7 hier."
Tinas Satz I've been here for 20 minutes entspricht „Ich bin seit 20 Minuten hier."
Im Englischen steht das Present Perfect, im Deutschen aber die Gegenwart. Außerdem heißt es im Englischen einmal since und einmal for – im Deutschen aber zweimal „seit".

Regel Im Englischen verwenden wir das Present Perfect (nicht die Gegenwart!), wenn wir sagen, wie lange ein Zustand schon andauert – ein Zustand, der in der Vergangenheit begonnen hat und bis in die Gegenwart andauert. Wir verwenden das Present Perfect …

– mit since, wenn wir den Anfangszeitpunkt nennen. Wenn wir sagen, seit wann etwas andauert.
– mit for, wenn wir die Zeitspanne nennen. Wenn wir sagen, wie lange etwas schon andauert.

We **have lived** (~~We live~~) here since 1995. *Wir wohnen seit 1995 hier.*
I've **known** (~~I know~~) her since my schooldays. *Ich kenne sie seit meiner Schulzeit.*
We **haven't seen** David since Christmas. *Wir haben David seit Weihnachten nicht mehr gesehen.*
I've **had** (~~I have~~) this jacket for over 10 years. *Ich habe diese Jacke seit über 10 Jahren.*
The car **has been** (~~The car is~~) there now for three weeks. *Das Auto ist jetzt seit drei Wochen dort.*
She's ill. She **hasn't been** to work for three weeks now. *Sie ist krank. Sie ist jetzt seit drei Wochen nicht mehr in der Arbeit gewesen.*

since + Anfangszeitpunkt
since 6 o'clock [Uhrzeit]
since breakfast [Tageszeit]
since Saturday [Wochentag]
since April [Monat]
since 1st January [Datum]
since 2001 [Jahreszahl]
since our holiday [Ereignis]

for + Zeitspanne
for 10 seconds / minutes / hours [Anzahl von Sekunden / Minuten / Stunden]
for three days / weeks / months [Anzahl von Tagen / Wochen / Monaten]
for 200 years [Anzahl von Jahren]
for ages *seit ewigen Zeiten*
for a long time *seit langem*

1. Ergänzen Sie **since** oder **for**.

a ________________ 1947
b ________________ two weeks
c ________________ yesterday
d ________________ half past two
e ________________ half an hour
f ________________ a day
g ________________ Wednesday
h ________________ 15 minutes
i ________________ 7.15
j ________________ three months
k ________________ April
l ________________ this morning

2. Korrigieren Sie. Dann übersetzen Sie die Sätze ins Deutsche.

a They ~~are~~ friends for many years. ________________
b We ~~know~~ each other since we were 15. ________________
c My mother ~~is~~ in hospital for more than two months. ________________
d Mrs Bolton ~~works~~ here for seven years. ________________
e Peter ~~is~~ in the Peking office since 1st April. ________________
f Bonnie ~~has~~ a terrible cold since the weekend. ________________
g I ~~watch~~ this programme every week since the beginning. ________________
____

3. Ergänzen Sie das Present Perfect und **since** oder **for**. Dann übersetzen Sie die Sätze.

a Sarah ________________ *(be)* on a diet ________________ last week.
b My partner and I ________________ *(be)* together ________________ three years now.
c They live in London now. They ________________ *(live)* there ________________ over a year.
d I ________________ *(know)* Ellen ________________ we were together in kindergarten!
e This ________________ *(happen)* three times ________________ they installed the new system.
f Last year they opened a new road. ________________ then, we ________________ *(use)* a different route.
g I ________________ *(not hear)* from Barry ________________ months.
h The children ________________ *(not watch)* any TV ________________ over a week now.
i It's a clever idea. They ________________ *(make)* money with it ________________ years now.

4. Übersetzen Sie.

a Wir kennen Peter Hollis seit 1999.
b Mrs Thomas arbeitet für uns seit sechs Monaten.
c Er ist seit Sonntag krank.
d Marys Mann ist seit mehreren *(several)* Jahren tot.
e Wir wissen seit langem von *(about)* dieser Organisation.
f Ich habe seit heute Morgen Kopfschmerzen.

24 How long have you known this?

Wie lange weißt du das schon?

How long have you known ...?

Das Verb in Tinas How long-Frage steht im Present Perfect. Im Deutschen hieße es „Wie lange weißt du das schon?“, also mit einer Gegenwartsform. In dieser Unit setzen wir das Thema aus Unit 23 fort: ein Andauern aus der Vergangenheit bis in die Gegenwart wird im Englischen mit dem Present Perfect ausgedrückt.

Regel Wenn wir fragen, wie lange ein Zustand schon andauert, verwenden wir How long ...? zusammen mit dem Present Perfect.

Die Antwort steht ebenfalls im Present Perfect und kann eine Zeitbestimmung mit since oder for (→ Unit 23) enthalten oder auch eine mit all (z. B. all my life, all day, all morning).

How long have you **lived** (~~do you live~~) here? *Wie lange wohnst du (schon) hier?*
– **I've lived** (~~I live~~) here all my life. *Ich wohne hier (schon) mein ganzes Leben (lang).*

How long has Mr Yasiko **worked** (~~does ... work~~) for Mitsubishi? *Wie lange arbeitet Herr Yasiko (schon) bei Mitsubishi?*
– He **has worked** (~~He works~~) there all his working life. *Er arbeitet schon sein ganzes Berufsleben (lang) dort.*

How long have you **felt** (~~do you feel~~) sick? *Wie lange fühlen Sie sich schon schlecht?*
– Well, **I've had** (~~I have~~) a migraine all day. *Nun, ich habe schon den ganzen Tag Migräne.*

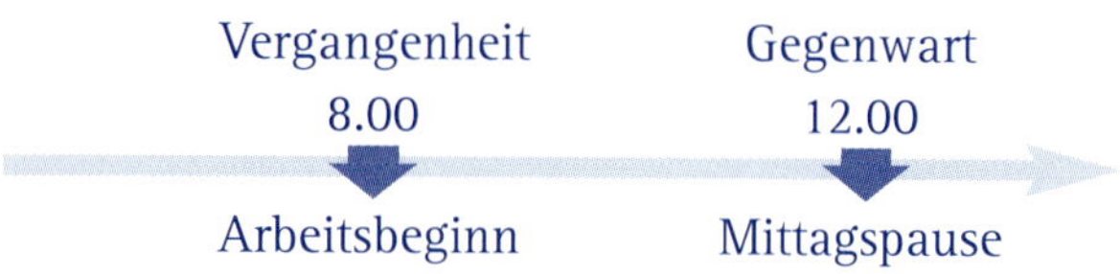

She **has been** at her desk since 8 o'clock.
She **has been** at her desk for four hours.
She **has been** at her desk all morning.

1. Korrigieren Sie. Setzen Sie das Verb ins Present Perfect.

a How long ~~do you know~~ Mr Ling? ______
b How long ~~is Alex~~ ill now? ______
c How long ~~are Peter and Jill~~ married now? ______
d How long ~~do you know~~ this? ______
e How long ~~do they have~~ this problem? ______
f How long ~~are you~~ back from your holiday? ______

2. Beantworten Sie die Fragen mit dem Present Perfect (+ since / for / all).

a How long have you known your best friend?
I've known my best friend ______
b How long have you lived where you live now?
I've lived in ______
c How long have you worked where you work now?
______
d How long have you had the shoes / jacket / jeans / ... that you now have on.
______
e How long have you used this book now?
______

3. Bilden Sie passende Fragen mit How long ...? und dem Present Perfect.

Tanja is away on holiday. – *How long has she been away?*
a Peter has a VW Beetle. – ______
b I know Annabelle. – ______
c We use a courier service. – ______
d They have a dog. – ______
e We live on an island. – ______
f Tom works in a hotel. – ______

4. Übersetzen Sie.

a Ich bin [schon][1] den ganzen Morgen [lang][1] hier.
b Tina ist [schon][1] die ganze Woche krank.
c Wie lange kennen Sie Mr Jameson [schon][1]?
d Wie lange fährt er diesen alten Ford [schon][1]?
e Wie lange hast du diese Wohnung [schon][1]?
f Ich kenne diesen Ort [schon][1] mein ganzes Leben [lang][1].

[1]Wörter in eckigen Klammern müssen nicht übersetzt werden.

25 I've been waiting since 6 o'clock.

Ich warte schon seit 6 Uhr.

I have been waiting ...

Tina wartet auf Tim. Sie wartet schon seit 18.00 Uhr. Das Warten begann in der Vergangenheit und dauert bis in die Gegenwart an, deshalb steht das Verb im Present Perfect (→ Units 23–24). have been waiting ist die Verlaufsform des Present Perfect.

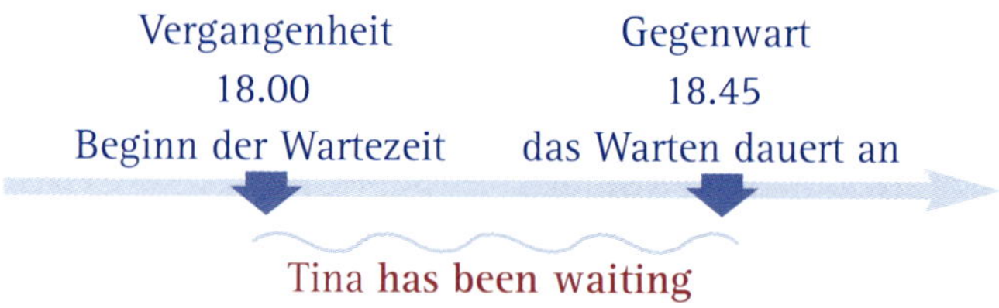

Regel Wenn wir sagen oder fragen, wie lange eine Handlung oder ein Vorgang schon andauert, verwenden wir die Verlaufsform des Present Perfect (Englisch: *present perfect continuous* oder *present perfect progressive*).
Diese Form bilden wir mit have / has been + -ing-Form des Verbs. Oft verwenden wir sie mit einer Zeitangabe wie since, for oder all.

Verlaufsform der Gegenwart	Verlaufsform des Present Perfect
I **am** waiting.	I **have been** waiting.
You / We / They **are** waiting.	You / We / They **have been** waiting.
He / She / It **is** waiting.	He / She / It **has been** waiting.

How long **has** Tina **been waiting**? *Wie lange wartet Tina schon?*
Tina **has been waiting** since 6.00. *Tina wartet (schon) seit 18.00 Uhr.*

How long **have** you **been learning** English? *Wie lange lernen Sie schon Englisch?*
I **have been learning** English for some time. *Ich lerne schon seit einiger Zeit Englisch.*

How long **has** it **been raining**? *Wie lange regnet es schon?*
It **has been raining** all morning. *Es regnet schon den ganzen Vormittag.*

1. Kreuzen Sie die richtige Form an.

a Angela … her homework since 6 o'clock.
- ☐ does
- ☐ has been doing

b He … on the phone for 50 minutes now.
- ☐ has been talking
- ☐ talks

c How long …?
- ☐ does it snow
- ☐ has it been snowing

d Sonia … six months.
- ☐ has been training for
- ☐ is training since

2. Bilden Sie Sätze zu dem Bild auf S. 60 mit der Verlaufsform des Present Perfect.

Tina / wait / since 6 o'clock *Tina has been waiting since 6 o'clock.*

a Tina / wait / for 45 minutes ______

b She / stand / in the cold all the time ______

c She / get / more and more angry ______

d Tim / sit / in a pub / since 5.30 ______

e He / talk / to an old friend ______

f They / drink / beer ______

3. Bilden Sie Fragen und Anworten mit der Verlaufsform des Present Perfect.

jog *How long has he been jogging?*
20 minutes *He has been jogging for 20 minutes.*

a 

read ______
2 hours ______

b 

study ______
35 minutes ______

c 

clean his car ______
40 minutes ______

d 

play tennis ______
1 hour ______

4. Übersetzen Sie ins Englische. Verwenden Sie die Verlaufsform des Present Perfect.

a I'm sorry I'm late. *Wie lange warten Sie [schon][1]?*

b Mrs Thomas is one of our best people. *Sie arbeitet seit August an* (on) *dem Projekt.*

c Listen. *Mrs Smiths Hund bellt* (bark) *[schon][1] den ganzen Abend.*

d Where can Mr Dawson be? *Wie lange versuchen wir [schon][1] ihn zu erreichen* (reach)*?*

e The weather's awful. *Es regnet [schon][1] die ganze Woche.*

f Let's stop for a break. *Wir fahren* (drive) *[schon][1] seit fünf Stunden.*

[1]Wörter in eckigen Klammern müssen nicht übersetzt werden.

Units 12–25

Wählen Sie die richtige Form.

Vergangenheitsform und Present Perfect

1. I ... at a great party last weekend.
   a) was
   b) were

2. You ... very late this morning. What happened?
   a) was
   b) were

3. Angela ... at work yesterday. She was ill.
   a) didn't be
   b) wasn't

4. We left early. We ... for the discussion.
   a) didn't stay
   b) stayed not

5. I ... to phone you, but you were out.
   a) tried
   b) tryed

6. I ... you. Where were you sitting?
   a) didn't saw
   b) didn't see

7. I ... tired all day yesterday.
   a) fall
   b) felt

8. We ... much sightseeing. There was so little time.
   a) didn't
   b) didn't do

9. What ... when you told him?
   a) said your boss
   b) did your boss say

10. What ... yesterday? – We spent the whole day on the beach.
    a) did you
    b) did you do

11. Where ... that beautiful blouse?
    a) bought you
    b) did you buy

12. I .... We had a drink together.
    a) met Peter yesterday
    b) met yesterday Peter

13. We ..., you know, 'Diabolo'. It's very good.
    a) tried last week that new restaurant
    b) tried that new restaurant last week

14. Your card was very quick. It arrived ....
    a) for two days
    b) two days ago

15. We saw Tony at the meeting. He ... to an Indian lady in a beautiful sari.
    a) talked
    b) was talking

16. I ... a bath when the phone rang, so I couldn't answer it.
    a) had
    b) was having

17. Have they ... the bill?
    a) paid
    b) payed

18. George and Liz ..., but all the others are here.
    a) hasn't come
    b) haven't come

19. Have you ... this sort of car before?
    a) ☐ driven
    b) ☐ drove

20. I ... Australia. People say it's a wonderful country.
    a) ☐ have never been to
    b) ☐ was never in

21. My sister ... New Zealand last year.
    a) ☐ has visited
    b) ☐ visited

22. Have you ...? – No, and I don't want to!
    a) ☐ eaten ever seaweed
    b) ☐ ever eaten seaweed

23. Mr Smith ... the company over two years ago.
    a) ☐ has left
    b) ☐ left

24. Have you ever been up in a hot-air balloon? – ...
    a) ☐ Yes, I've.
    b) ☐ Yes, I have.

25. We haven't seen Andrea much ... .
    a) ☐ in the last time
    b) ☐ lately

26. I've spent ...!
    a) ☐ already over $1000
    b) ☐ over $1000 already

27. I ... the book last year on holiday. The film is not so good.
    a) ☐ have read
    b) ☐ read

28. How was the journey? When ...?
    a) ☐ did you arrive
    b) ☐ have you arrived

29. They ... together since last year. They met at evening classes.
    a) ☐ are
    b) ☐ have been

30. I ... 10 years now.
    a) ☐ am working here since
    b) ☐ have been working here for

Vergleichen Sie nun Ihre Lösungen mit dem Schlüssel auf S. 156. Wenn Sie Aufgaben nicht richtig gelöst haben, wiederholen Sie noch einmal die betreffende Unit. Diese Tabelle zeigt Ihnen, auf welche Unit sich die einzelnen Aufgaben beziehen.

Aufgabe	Unit	Aufgabe	Unit
1	12	16	18
2	12	17	19
3	13	18	19
4	13	19	19
5	13	20	20
6	14	21	20
7	14	22	20
8	14	23	20
9	15	24	20
10	15	25	21
11	15	26	21
12	16	27	22
13	16	28	22
14	16	29	23
15	17	30	25

26 He used to give me red roses.

Früher hat er mir immer rote Rosen geschenkt.

he used to give ...

Früher mal – in den ersten Jahren der Beziehung wohl – hat Tim immer rote Rosen geschenkt. Jetzt tut er es nicht mehr. Mit dem etwas eigentümlichen Ausdruck used to ... drückt Tina aus, was ihr Partner früher öfter getan hat und nun nicht mehr tut.

Regel Mit used to + Infinitiv (= Grundform des Verbs) drücken wir aus, was jemand früher öfter, regelmäßig oder gewohnheitsmäßig getan hat – aber jetzt nicht mehr tut.
Die Form used to ist für alle Personen gleich.
Frage und Verneinung bilden wir mit did(n't).

I / We You They He / She	**used to** **didn't use to**	smoke.	**Did**	I / we you they he /she	**use to smoke?**

I **used to smoke**, but I stopped last year. *Ich habe früher geraucht, aber ich habe letztes Jahr aufgehört.*

When we were children, we **used to play** cowboys and Indians. *Als wir Kinder waren, spielten wir Cowboys und Indianer.*

Jackie **used to have** long hair. But I like it short. *Jackie hatte früher immer lange Haare. Aber kurz gefallen sie mir.*

I **didn't use to like** Fiona, but now I think she's quite nice. *Ich mochte Fiona früher nicht, aber jetzt finde ich sie ganz nett.*

Where **did** you **use to work** before you started here? *Wo haben Sie früher gearbeitet, bevor Sie hier anfingen?*

1. Kreuzen Sie die richtige Form an.

a I … play squash, but I've given up.
- use to
- used to

b Look. There are Dave and Jenny – with a dog. They … have a dog, I'm sure.
- didn't use to
- used not

c He looks different somehow. … have a beard?
- Did he use to
- Used he

d Where … live before you came here?
- did you use to
- did you used

e He … me every week when he worked in New Zealand.
- use to phone
- used to phone

f This seems expensive. It … cost so much.
- not used to
- didn't use to

2. Bilden Sie Sätze wie im Beispiel.

Tony *used to smoke* cheap cigarettes. Now he smokes Havana cigars.

a He ______________________ an old Fiat. Now he drives a BMW.
b He ______________________ in a one-room flat. Now he lives in a big house.
c He ______________________ at McDonald's at weekends. Now he works 70 hours a week for his own firm.
d He ______________________ cheap red wine. Now he drinks champagne.
e He ______________________ lots of fun. Now he has time for nothing but work.
f He ______________________ in a band. Now he doesn't play anything.
g He ______________________ happy. Now he is always stressed.

3. Übersetzen Sie. Verwenden Sie **used to**.

a *Früher haben wir [immer][1] in Castle Street geparkt.* But we can't now.
b *Früher mochte ich Sonias Mann nicht.* Now I think he's sweet.
c *Früher hatten Familien nur ein Fernsehgerät.* Now they often have two or three.
d *Früher haben wir [immer][1] per* (by) *Brief bestellt.* Now we do it online.
e *Früher war Lachs* (salmon) *ein teurer Fisch.* But it isn't expensive now.
f *Wo haben Sie früher gewohnt?* Before you came here.

[1] Wörter in eckigen Klammern müssen nicht übersetzt werden.

4. Schreiben Sie auf ein Blatt, was Sie früher gemacht bzw. nicht gemacht haben.

play the piano / with Barbie dolls / … • have long / short / blond / … hair • like milk / bananas / ketchup with … / chocolate / … • go to … for my holidays • have a pet / friend called … • be in a … club • be afraid of big dogs / the dark / …

Beispiele:

Was ich früher gemacht habe, aber jetzt nicht mehr mache:
I used to play the piano.

Was ich früher nicht gemacht habe, aber jetzt mache:
I didn't use to have short hair.

27

I had fallen asleep.

Ich war eingeschlafen.

I had fallen asleep ...

Tina erzählt jetzt (3) von der vergangenen Nacht. Als Tim von seiner Feier nach Hause kam (2), war sie bereits lange vor dem Fernseher eingeschlafen (1). Diese zeitlichen Bezüge drückt Tina durch unterschiedliche Verbformen aus.

1	2	3
00.00 Uhr	02.00 Uhr	10.00 Uhr
Tina eingeschlafen	Tim nach Hause	Tina telefoniert
Vorvergangenheit	Vergangenheit	Gegenwart
had fallen asleep	came, woke	is up

Regel Wir verwenden had + Partizip Perfekt, um auszudrücken, dass etwas bereits vor einem in der Vergangenheit liegenden Zeitpunkt abgeschlossen war. had ist für alle Personen gleich. Diese Form nennen wir Vorvergangenheit oder Plusquamperfekt (Englisch: *past perfect*).

I / You / We / They	**had started.**	I / You / We / They	**had not finished.**
He / She / It	**had started.**	He / She / It	**had not finished.**

When we got to the station, the train **had** already **left.** *Als wir zum Bahnhof kamen, war der Zug bereits abgefahren.*

When I spoke to Bill, someone **had** already **informed** him. *Als ich mit Bill sprach, hatte ihn jemand bereits informiert.*

I wanted to start the meeting, but they **hadn't prepared** the room. *Ich wollte mit der Sitzung beginnen, aber sie hatten den Raum nicht vorbereitet.*

Die Kurzform von had ist 'd.

He finally found the keys. They**'d been** in his pocket all the time. *Er fand schließlich die Schlüssel. Sie waren die ganze Zeit in seiner Tasche gewesen.*

1. Ergänzen Sie **had** + Partizip Perfekt.

a I phoned Jim, but he ______________________ *(already leave)* the house.
b When I arrived home, my children ______________________ *(already cook)* supper.
c The police ______________________ *(arrive)* and an ambulance was there, too.
d I had to wake my husband up. He ______________________ *(fall)* asleep in front of the TV.
e When she left, Mrs Philips ______________________ *(work)* here over 20 years.
f I was so angry and went home. He ______________________ *(forget)* our date!
g The restaurant was full, but we were lucky because Ann ______________________ *(reserve)* a table.

2. Bilden Sie Sätze mit **had** + Partizip Perfekt.

Familie Trilling fuhr letztes Wochenende in Urlaub. Als sie abends ankam, waren alle k.o.
(drive 700 kilometres) *They had driven 700 kilometres.*

a *(see two accidents)* ______________________
b *(stand in a traffic jam for two hours)* ______________________
c *(have a breakdown)* ______________________
d *(lose their way twice)* ______________________
e *(leave the hotel address at home)* ______________________

3. Schreiben Sie Sätze mit **hadn't** + Partizip Perfekt und **before** wie im Beispiel.

In France last year I went surfing. *I hadn't surfed before* *(surf)*.

a I had guests yesterday. I gave them paella. ______________________ *(cook that)*.
b On holiday last year we ate some raw fish. ______________________ *(eat that)*.
c Ann introduced me to her parents last week. ______________________ *(meet them)*.
d Jackie took me to a ballet last Monday. ______________________ *(be to one)*.
e Sonia at the health club gave me an Indian massage. ______________________ *(have one)*.
f At Debbie's wedding last month I wore the dress I bought in Thailand. ______________________ *(wear it)*.

4. Übersetzen Sie. Verwenden Sie **had** + Partizip Perfekt.

a I got to the airport late. *Tims Maschine* (plane) *war schon gelandet.*
b David phoned Anita. *Aber jemand hatte sie schon informiert.*
c We knew the book. *Aber wir hatten den Film nicht gesehen.*
d Jonathan phoned in a panic from the airport. *Er hatte seinen Pass vergessen.*
e Elizabeth gave a big party. *Sie hatte € 500 im Lotto* (on the lottery) *gewonnen.*
f I was tired. *Ich hatte nicht viel geschlafen.*

28 I'm just going to check the football results.

Ich will gerade die Fußballergebnisse nachschauen.

I'm going to ... We're going to ...

Mit I'm just going to check the football results drückt Tim eine Absicht aus. Mit ihrer Warnung We're going to be late drückt Tina aus, was sie kommen sieht – dass sie sich verspäten. Unser Cartoon zeigt Beispiele für die zwei unterschiedlichen Verwendungen von going to.

Regel Mit be going to + Infinitiv (= Grundform des Verbs) drücken wir aus, dass wir etwas tun wollen – jetzt gleich oder später.

be going to = Absicht, Vorhaben, Entschluss, Plan

I	am	Am I
You / We / They	are (not) **going to eat** now.	Are you / we / they **going to eat?**
He / She / It	is	Is he / she / it

Philip **is going to phone** this evening about 9. *Philip will heute Abend gegen 9 anrufen.*
I'**m going to watch** the news. *Ich will (gleich) die Nachrichten anschauen.*
What's his name? – I'**m not going to tell** you. ... *Das sage ich dir nicht.*
Sandra is so angry. She **is not going to pay**. ... *Sie will nicht bezahlen.*
Are you **going to drive** or **come** by train? *Wollt ihr mit dem Auto oder mit dem Zug kommen?*

Mit be going to drücken wir auch aus, was wir kommen sehen, d. h. was aufgrund von Vorzeichen geschehen wird.

be going to = an Gewissheit grenzende Erwartung

We'**re going to be** late. *Wir kommen zu spät.*
Look at those clouds. It'**s going to rain**. *Schau dir diese Wolken an. Es regnet gleich.*
Oh no! There'**s going to be** an accident. *Oh nein! Da passiert gleich ein Unfall.*

1. Ergänzen Sie die passende Form von be going to.

a We've been out three times this week. This evening we ______________________ *(stay)* at home.

b David has decided not to have a holiday in the summer. He ______________________ *(wait)* till September.

c Sonia ______________________ *(sell)* her car. She doesn't need one now.

d They've offered John the job and he ______________________ *(take)* it.

e They are a strong team, but we ______________________ *(win)*!

f I've decided I can't do it alone. I ______________________ *(ask)* Peter for help.

g Dave and Marlis are coming to dinner. I ______________________ *(make)* paella.

h There's a message from Transco. Mrs Baxter ______________________ *(phone)* you tomorrow.

i Can I drive you to the airport? – No, thanks. Our son ______________________ *(drive)* us.

j Do you need a hotel? – No, we ______________________ *(stay)* with friends.

2. Drücken Sie eine Weigerung mit I'm not going to ... aus.

They want €250. *I am not going to pay* *(pay)* that!

a Mr Wills wants some coffee. I ______________________ *(make)* it. Why should I?

b Someone has to work this weekend. – I ______________________ *(offer)*.

c Where have you been? – I ______________________ *(tell)* you.

d Who can feed the cat for me? – I ______________________ *(do)* it.

e He says we have to pay for the repair. – I ______________________ *(agree)* to that.

3. Wie lautet die Frage?

I am going to watch XXXXX. – Sorry? What *are you going to watch?*

a I am going to invite XXXXX. – Sorry? Who ______________________?

b I'm going to wear XXXXX tonight. – Sorry? What ______________________?

c I'm going to see XXXXX. – Sorry? Which film ______________________?

d I'm going to park XXXXX. – Sorry? Where ______________________?

e I'm going to give her XXX for her birthday. – Sorry? What ______________________?

4. Was geschieht gleich? Schreiben Sie einen Satz mit be going to.

a 

b 

c 

d 

a it / rain ______________________

b train / leave ______________________

c she / have a baby ______________________

d bus / stop ______________________

29 I'm meeting Bill at the pub at 8.

Ich bin um 8 mit Bill in der Kneipe verabredet.

I'm meeting …

Der Cartoontext enthält zwei Verben in der Verlaufsform der Gegenwart: are you going und I'm meeting. In den Units 6–10 haben wir gelernt, dass man mit dieser Form einen Vorgang beschreibt, der gerade im Verlauf begriffen ist. Das trifft hier für are you going zu, denn Tim ist gerade im Begriff wegzugehen. I'm meeting ist jedoch kein Vorgang, der gerade im Verlauf begriffen ist, sondern bezieht sich auf ein zukünftiges Ereignis.
In dieser Unit beschäftigen wir uns mit einer weiteren Anwendung der Verlaufsform der Gegenwart – zum Ausdruck der Zukunft.

Regel Mit der Verlaufsform der Gegenwart drücken wir aus, dass etwas für die Zukunft ausgemacht ist. Es liegt eine bestimmte Zeitplanung vor, Vorkehrungen und Abmachungen sind getroffen.

My friend Ann **is getting married** on 17th April. *Meine Freundin Ann heiratet am 17. April.*
Tom **is taking** his driving test next Friday morning. *Nächsten Freitagmorgen macht Tom seine Fahrprüfung.*
We're **having** dinner together tomorrow. *Morgen essen wir zusammen zu Abend.*
What **are** you **doing** this weekend? *Was machst du kommendes Wochenende?*

Wenn wir von einer Abmachung für die Zukunft sprechen, verwenden wir die Verlaufsform der Gegenwart in aller Regel mit einer entsprechenden Zeitangabe: tomorrow, next week, on Thursday usw.

1. Ergänzen Sie die passende Form der Verlaufsform der Gegenwart.

a Tom ______________________ *(come)* to supper tomorrow.
b I ______________________ *(meet)* Susanne for a drink after work tonight.
c We ______________________ *(go)* skiing at the weekend. Do you want to come?
d It's Dave's birthday next month. He ______________________ *(give)* a big party.
e What ______________________ *(you / do)* this Sunday? Can we meet?
f When ______________________ *(you / leave)* for Paris? – Straight after work on Friday.
g What time ______________________ *(we / meet)* tonight? At 7.30 or at 8?
h How ______________________ *(you / go)* to the party tomorrow?

2. Schreiben Sie, was Christine diese Woche für Termine hat.

Sunday	Monday	Tuesday	Wednesday	Thursday	Friday	Saturday
~~Jack and Dora here~~	~~16.00 meeting~~	work: 9.00–15.00 evening: cinema with Jill	10.00 dentist evening: cook for Mike's birthday party	lunch with Mum work: 15.00–21.00	11.00 tennis with Adrian 20.00 sauna	work: 9.00–16.00

It is Monday evening.
(work) Tomorrow *she is working from 9 till 3.*
a *(go)* Tomorrow evening ______________________
b *(go)* On Wednesday ______________________
c *(cook)* On Wednesday evening ______________________
d *(have)* On Thursday ______________________
e *(work)* On Thursday ______________________
f *(play)* On Friday morning ______________________
g *(go)* On Friday evening ______________________
h *(work)* On Saturday ______________________

3. Bilden Sie Fragen wie im Beispiel.

what / you / do / this coming Friday *What are you doing this coming Friday?*
a where / the club committee / meet / tomorrow evening ______________________
____
b when / we / play / next Saturday ______________________
c what time / we / see / the Smiths / next Sunday ______________________
____
d when / Andrew / fetch / these chairs ______________________
e what day / your mother / arrive ______________________
f when / they / deliver / the new fax machine ______________________

30 You won't notice it.
Sie werden es nicht merken.

will ... won't

Der Zahnarzt ist überzeugt: alles wird in Ordnung sein, Tim wird den Eingriff nicht merken. Mit will und won't drückt der Zahnarzt aus, was in Zukunft (nicht) sein wird – wenn Tim erstmal den Mund aufgemacht hat.

Regel Mit will und won't + Infinitiv (= Grundform des Verbs) sagen wir, was in der Zukunft eintreten bzw. nicht eintreten wird. will und won't sind für alle Personen gleich.
will hat die Kurzform 'll; diese wird oft nach einem Pronomen gebraucht.
won't ist die Kurzform von will not.
(Weitere Hinweise, auch zum Unterschied zwischen will und going to, folgen in Unit 31.)

I / You We / They He / She / It	**will be** there soon.

I / You We / They He / She / It	**won't be** late.

Our friends from Chicago **will be** here next week. *Unsere Freunde aus Chicago werden nächste Woche hier sein.*
Prices **will rise** next year by 3 %. *Die Preise werden nächstes Jahr um 3 % steigen.*
I'll **try** to find out tomorrow, but **it won't be** easy. *Ich werde versuchen das morgen herauszufinden, aber es wird nicht leicht sein.*
Will Christine **be** at the party? *Wird Christine auf der Party sein?*
When **will** I **see** you again? *Wann werde ich dich wiedersehen?*

! will entspricht deutsch „werden". Deutsch „wollen" dagegen entspricht want(s) (to).
Sandra will Kaffee, nicht Tee. = Sandra **wants** (~~will~~) coffee, not tea.
Ich will den Gesamtpreis wissen. = I **want to** (~~will~~) know the total price.

! Im Deutschen kann die Zukunft oft mit einer Gegenwartsform ausgedrückt werden. Im Englischen ist oft nur eine Zukunftsform möglich.
Sag ihm, ich bin bald zurück. = Tell him I **will be** (~~I am~~) back soon.
Morgen wissen wir mehr. = We'll **know** (~~We know~~) more tomorrow.

1. Kreuzen Sie die richtige Form an.

a My son … a dog.
- ☐ wants
- ☐ will

b Dave can help us. He … back soon.
- ☐ is
- ☐ will be

c Drive slower! I … have an accident.
- ☐ don't want to
- ☐ won't

d Please wait here. The doctor … you in a minute.
- ☐ sees
- ☐ will see

e If we don't hurry, we … our train!
- ☐ miss
- ☐ will miss

f Hurry up! The teacher … start.
- ☐ wants to
- ☐ will

2. Korrigieren Sie. Setzen Sie eine Zukunftsform mit will ein.

You don't have to leave now. Peter ~~drives~~ you home later.
Peter will drive you home later.

a Can I speak to Mrs Simson, please? – One moment, please. I ~~put~~ you through.
____

b Come this way, please. I ~~show~~ you your room. ____________________

c I think Mark ~~phones~~ later this evening. ____________________

d Quick, or they ~~close~~. ____________________

e Would you like a cup of coffee while you wait? Mrs Wilkins ~~is~~ here very soon.
____

f My son is so lazy. I'm afraid he ~~fails~~ his final exam. ____________________

3. Ergänzen Sie. Verwenden Sie will und won't.

a My father ____________ *(be)* 60 next year.
b I'm sure you ____________ *(enjoy)* it. Cora's parties are always great.
c I don't think it ____________ *(snow)*. It's not cold enough.
d I'm sorry, but we ____________ *(not know)* the exact details before next week.
e Don't worry. The repair ____________ *(not be)* too expensive.
f They've had a big fire at their house. – Oh no! What ____________ *(they / do)*?
Where ____________ *(they / go)*?

4. Übersetzen Sie. Verwenden Sie will und won't.

a Du wirst sehen: wir gewinnen am Samstag.
b Morgen wissen wir mehr.
c Mr Baker ruft morgen zurück.
d Morgen fühlt er [sich][1] viel besser.
e Sally ist in fünf Minuten hier.
f In Zukunft werde ich vorsichtiger *(more careful)* sein. Es passiert nicht wieder.

[1]Das Wort in eckigen Klammern muss nicht übersetzt werden.

31 I think I'll have champagne.

Ich glaube, ich nehme Champagner.

I think I'll have ...

Tina verwendet die Zukunftsform I'll have (nicht: ~~I have~~) nach I think, was sehr häufig der Fall ist. Die Zukunftsform verwendet sie auch deshalb, weil sie sich spontan im Augenblick für Champagner entscheidet. In dieser Unit geht es um weitere Besonderheiten beim Gebrauch von will / won't (→ Unit 30).

Regel will und won't verwenden wir oft nach I (don't) think (ich glaube [nicht]), I hope (ich hoffe), I expect (ich rechne damit), I'm certain / sure (ich bin mir sicher) und I'm afraid (ich fürchte).

I think Sonia **will find** her new job very interesting. *Ich glaube, Sonia wird ihre neue Stelle sehr interessant finden.*

I hope we'**ll have** time to see Soho. *Ich hoffe, wir werden genug Zeit haben, um Soho zu sehen.*

I expect they'**ll tell** us at the meeting tomorrow. *Ich rechne damit, dass sie es uns morgen auf der Sitzung sagen werden.*

I'm certain / sure it **won't happen** before next year. *Ich bin mir sicher, dass es nicht vor nächstem Jahr passiert.*

I'm afraid I **won't be** there. *Ich fürchte, ich werde nicht da sein.*

will / won't verwenden wir für spontane Entschlüsse und Angebote – going to oder die Verlaufsform der Gegenwart dagegen für solche, die vorüberlegt sind (→ Units 28–29).

I'**ll carry** that. *Das trage ich.*

Wait. I'**ll get** a plaster. *Warte. Ich hole ein Pflaster.*

... is not here. – OK, I'**ll call** again later. *OK, ich rufe später wieder an.*

Aber:

It's Deborah's 30th birthday soon. She **is going to have** a big party at the Hilton. *Sie will eine große Party im Hilton feiern.*

I'**m meeting** David tomorrow night. *Ich treffe mich morgen Abend mit David.*

1. Ergänzen Sie die will-Zukunft.

a I think ______________________ *(I / wait)* till the others are ready.
b I don't think ______________________ *(we / find out)* much from the neighbours.
c I expect ______________________ *(Richard / be)* at the party.
d I'm sure ______________________ *(the police / find)* it.
e I'm afraid ______________________ *(we / miss)* our train.
f I hope ______________________ *(it / not rain).*

2. Machen Sie Angebote mit I'll . . . .

We ought to book a table. – *(do)* I'll do it.
a Perhaps Philip knows the address. – *(ask)* ______________________
b This bag is so heavy. – *(carry)* ______________________ for you.
c Does anybody want this last sandwich? – *(eat)* ______________________
d It's very hot in here. – *(open)* ______________________ the window.
e Let's have a break. – *(make)* ______________________ some coffee.
f It's time to go, but Dave isn't here. – *(wait)* ______________________

3. Spontaner Entschluss (will) oder vorüberlegter Entschluss (going to)? Ergänzen Sie.

a We decided a long time ago. We ______________________ *(stay)* here at Christmas.
b We have to agree who pays for what. I ______________________ *(buy)* the wine.
c It's been such a hard day, I don't want to cook now. Come on, we ______________________ *(eat)* out.
d Tony booked a table at the Green Dragon. They ______________________ *(give)* us a table by the window.
e Sorry, I forgot. I ______________________ *(do)* it tomorrow.
f The course is very expensive, but I've thought about it and I ______________________ *(do)* it.

4. Übersetzen Sie. Verwenden Sie will.

a Wait. *Ich helfe dir.*
b The Spanish team is very good. *Ich glaube, wir verlieren am Samstag.*
c It's not far. *Ich zeige Ihnen den Weg.*
d What would you like? – *Ich nehme* (have) *den Fisch bitte.*
e She's not answering the phone. *Ich schicke ihr eine E-Mail.*
f I'm sorry, but I don't have any money with me. – *Kein Problem, ich bezahle.*

This was made in China.

Das wurde in China hergestellt.

[1] echt

Made in China

Made in … ist grammatisch gesehen eine verkürzte Form des Passiv-Satzes This was made in … (= Das wurde in … hergestellt). In der Grammatik unterscheiden wir zwischen Aktivsätzen und Passivsätzen. In einem Aktivsatz wird gesagt, wer etwas tut, z. B. **Lisa** bakes wonderful cakes (Lisa backt wunderbare Kuchen). In einem Passivsatz wird gesagt, was mit jemandem oder etwas getan wird / wurde, z. B. **This cake** was baked yesterday (**Dieser Kuchen** wurde gestern gebacken). In dieser und der nächsten Unit beschäftigen wir uns mit Passivsätzen im Englischen.

Regel Das Passiv bilden wir mit einer Form von be + Partizip Perfekt.

1. **Gegenwart:** am / is / are + Partizip Perfekt

Aktiv People in Canada **speak** English. *Die Menschen in Kanada sprechen Englisch.*
Passiv English **is spoken** in Canada. *In Kanada wird Englisch gesprochen.*

Aktiv People often **eat** chips with ketchup. *Leute essen Pommes frites oft mit Ketchup.*
Passiv Chips **are** often **eaten** with ketchup. *Pommes frites werden oft mit Ketchup gegessen.*

2. **Vergangenheit:** was / were + Partizip Perfekt

Aktiv They **arrested** a man yesterday. *Sie haben gestern einen Mann verhaftet.*
Passiv A man **was arrested** yesterday. *Ein Mann wurde gestern verhaftet.*

Aktiv They **built** these houses in 1980. *Man hat diese Häuser 1980 gebaut.*
Passiv These houses **were built** in 1980. *Diese Häuser wurden 1980 gebaut.*

Nach will oder einem Modalverb (can, must usw.) verwenden wir die Passivform des Infinitivs. Diese heißt einheitlich be + Partizip Perfekt.

Aktiv Someone *will* **inform** you. *Jemand wird Sie informieren.*
Passiv You *will* **be informed**. *Sie werden informiert werden.*

Aktiv You *must* **shut** the windows. *Sie müssen die Fenster schließen.*
Passiv The windows *must* **be shut**. *Die Fenster müssen geschlossen werden.*

1. Kreuzen Sie die richtige Form an.

a Wine ... in bottles.
- ☐ is sell
- ☐ is sold

b The bill ... yesterday evening.
- ☐ is paid
- ☐ was paid

c The new sofa ... tomorrow.
- ☐ will be delivered
- ☐ will deliver

d These books ... yesterday.
- ☐ are ordered
- ☐ were ordered

e Reserved tickets ... before 7.30.
- ☐ must be collected
- ☐ must collected

f Euros ... everywhere.
- ☐ isn't accepted
- ☐ aren't accepted

2. Ergänzen Sie die Gegenwartsform des Passivs.

a English ______________________ *(speak)* in many different countries.
b White wine ______________________ *(drink)* at a lower temperature than red.
c Beer ______________________ *(sell)* in bottles or cans.
d Passengers ______________________ *(ask)* not to smoke.
e As a star, I ______________________ *(know)* all over the world.
f In England presents ______________________ *(give)* on the morning of December 25th.
g Cheese ______________________ *(make)* from milk.

3. Verwandeln Sie in einen Passivsatz in der Vergangenheit.

(We) sent the goods yesterday. ➡ *The goods were sent yesterday.*
a *(Someone)* saw the thief. ➡ ______________________
b *(The police)* arrested two men last night. ➡ ______________________
c *(They)* sold over 50000 CDs on the first day. ➡ ______________________
d *(The author)* wrote the book in 1928. ➡ ______________________
e *(They)* killed over 3000 civilians. ➡ ______________________
f *(They)* opened the new museum last year. ➡ ______________________

4. Übersetzen Sie. Verwenden Sie die Infinitivform des Passivs.

a Bags ______________________ *(können hinterlassen werden)* at reception.
b Bills ______________________ *(müssen bezahlt werden)* at once.
c Everybody ______________________ *(wird informiert werden)* by e-mail or by phone.
d Brochures ______________________ *(können bestellt werden)* online.
e Cars ______________________ *(müssen geparkt werden)* in the official car-park.
f The box ______________________ *(kann benutzt werden)* again.

33 We are being terrorized.
Wir werden terrorisiert.

... are being ...ed

Tim hat das Gefühl, dass er und Tina von Reklamepost-Verschickern terrorisiert werden. Er bringt das zum Ausdruck mit der Form are being + Partizip Perfekt. Es handelt sich um die Verlaufsform der Gegenwart im Passiv. In dieser Unit geht es um weitere Zeitformen des Passivs.

Regel Die Verlaufsform des Passivs bilden wir mit einer Form von be + being + Partizip Perfekt. Der Gebrauchsunterschied zur einfachen Form entspricht dem in Aktivsätzen (→ Units 9–11, 17–18).

Aktiv They **are treating** me well. *Sie behandeln mich gut.*
Passiv I **am being treated** well. *Ich werde gut behandelt.*

Aktiv Someone **is watching** us. *Jemand beobachtet uns.*
Passiv We **are being watched**. *Wir werden beobachtet.*

Einfache Form: 'Dinner for One' **is shown** *every year.*
„Dinner for One" wird jedes Jahr gezeigt.
Verlaufsform: *At the moment* adverts **are being shown.**
Im Augenblick werden Werbespots gezeigt.

Das Passiv des Present Perfect bilden wir mit have / has + been + Partizip Perfekt. Der Gebrauchsunterschied zur Vergangenheitsform entspricht dem in Aktivsätzen (→ Units 20–22).

Aktiv They've **invited** the Smiths too. *Sie haben auch die Smiths eingeladen.*
Passiv The Smiths **have been invited** too. *Die Smiths sind auch eingeladen worden.*

Aktiv Someone **has stolen** my bike! *Jemand hat mein Rad gestohlen!*
Passiv My bike **has been stolen**. *Mein Rad ist gestohlen worden.*

Present Perfect: We **have been informed.** [= We know *now.*] *Wir sind informiert worden.*
Vergangenheit: We **were informed** *last week.* *Wir wurden letzte Woche informiert.*

1. Kreuzen Sie die richtige Form an.

a My camera … .
- ☐ is stolen
- ☐ has been stolen

b Our house … this week.
- ☐ is being painted
- ☐ is painted

c The bill … .
- ☐ is been paid
- ☐ has been paid

d A new hotel … . It will open next year.
- ☐ is built
- ☐ is being built

e The invitations … today.
- ☐ are being sent out
- ☐ are sent out

f My colleague … .
- ☐ has fired
- ☐ has been fired

2. Ergänzen Sie die Verlaufsform der Gegenwart im Passiv.

a A new model ________________ *(develop)*.
b A new hospital ________________ *(build)* outside the town.
c The road outside our hotel ________________ *(repair)*. The noise is awful!
d Who ________________ *(interview)* at the moment? Which candidate?
e Two car drivers ________________ *(treat)* in hospital after the accident.
f What ________________ *(say)*? I can't hear.

3. Verwandeln Sie in einen Passivsatz im Present Perfect.

(They) haven't invited me. ➡ *I haven't been invited*.
a *(They)* have sold all the tickets. ➡ ________________
b *(Someone)* has found the keys. ➡ ________________
c *(They)* have informed us. ➡ We ________________
d *(Someone)* has already made coffee. ➡ ________________
e *(Someone)* has booked the whole restaurant. ➡ ________________
f *(They)* have asked me to help. ➡ I ________________

4. Übersetzen Sie. Verwenden Sie die Verlaufsform der Gegenwart oder das Present Perfect im Passiv.

a Our car ________________ *(ist gestohlen worden)*.
b Which part of the building ________________ *(wird geputzt)* today?
c My friends ________________ *(sind nicht eingeladen worden)*.
d Which scene ________________ *(wird gedreht[1])* today?
e The firm ________________ *(ist verkauft worden)*.
f Oh look, our new sofa ________________ *(wird [gerade][2] geliefert)*.

[1] film
[2] Wörter in eckigen Klammern müssen nicht übersetzt werden.

34 The photo was taken by Tim.

Das Foto wurde von Tim gemacht.

… was taken by …

Beachten Sie die Präposition: The photo was taken by Tim (Das Foto wurde von Tim gemacht). Die falsche Wiedergabe von deutsch „von" (mit ~~from~~ – richtig aber: by) ist eine häufige Fehlerquelle in englischen Passivsätzen. In solchen Sätzen wird die handelnde Person (der so genannte Urheber) meist nicht genannt, weil sie unbekannt oder unwichtig ist. Wird sie doch genannt, dann mit by.

Regel In einem Passivsatz können wir den *Urheber* der Handlung mit by nennen.

Aktiv *Lisa* **baked** this cake. *Lisa hat diesen Kuchen gebacken.*

Passiv This cake **was baked by** *Lisa*. *Dieser Kuchen wurde von Lisa gebacken.*

Wir fragen nach dem Urheber mit Who … by? Dabei steht by am Satzende, nicht am Satzanfang.

Who was the photo taken **by**? *Von wem wurde das Foto gemacht?*

Who were the sandwiches made **by**? *Von wem wurden die Butterbrote gemacht?*

1. Korrigieren Sie.

a The match was won ~~from~~ Bayern Munich. ______________________

b Who was this book written ~~from~~? ______________________

c The ceremony was watched ~~from~~ millions on TV. ______________________

d His father was killed ~~from~~ a terrorist. ______________________

e Who was this picture painted ~~from~~? ______________________

f Who were you invited ~~from~~? ______________________

2. Verwandeln Sie ins Passiv.

Ann wrote this story. ➡ *This story was written by Ann*.

a Tony sent this fax. ➡ ______________________

b A neighbour fed our cat. ➡ ______________________

c My secretary chose the hotel. ➡ ______________________

d An Australian teaches the Italian course. ➡ ______________________

e Two boys saw the thief. ➡ ______________________

f My son installed our computer. ➡ ______________________

3. Bilden Sie Passivfragen in der Vergangenheit.

Who / this picture / paint? – Picasso.

Who was this picture painted by? – Picasso.

a Who / President Kennedy / kill?

______________________ – By Lee Harvey Oswald, probably.

b Who / the first computer / make?

______________________ – I don't know. Was it Bill Gates?

c Who / the letter / sign?

______________________ – By the Vice-President.

d Who / you / invite?

______________________ – By Ann. She and I are colleagues.

e Who / the gold medal / win?

______________________ – By Finland. They were very good.

f Who / you / inform?

______________________ – By my boss. He told me yesterday.

4. Übersetzen Sie. Achten Sie auf die Zeit: Gegenwart oder Vergangenheit?

a Von wem wurde er informiert?

b Von wem wirst du bezahlt?

c Die Party wurde von den Eltern organisiert.

d Englisch wird von Millionen von Menschen gesprochen.

e Ich werde immer von meinem Sohn aufgeweckt.

f Das Buch wurde von einem Amerikaner geschrieben.

35 Who did you meet?

Wen hast du getroffen?

Who did you ...?

Zu dem Satz Tim met a snowman („Tim ist einem Schneemann begegnet") kann man zwei Fragen mit who stellen:

1. Who did Tim meet? (Antwort: A snowman.) *Wem ist Tim begegnet?*
2. Who met a snowman? (Antwort: Tim.) *Wer ist einem Schneemann begegnet?*

In Frage 1 entspricht who dem deutschen „wen" bzw. „wem". In solchen Fragen kommt eine Form des Hilfsverbs do zum Einsatz (hier: did). Deshalb fragt Tina: Who **did** you meet?
In Frage 2 entspricht who dem deutschen „wer"; did kommt nicht zum Einsatz.

Regel who-Fragen, in denen who „wen / wem" entspricht, bilden wir mit do, does oder did – wenn sonst kein Hilfsverb vorhanden ist (z. B. have, will, is / are / was / were).
who-Fragen, in denen who „wer" entspricht, bilden wir ohne das Hilfsverb do.

Tim and Tina hate the Smiths. *Tim und Tina hassen die Smiths.*
Who **do** Tim and Tina **hate**? – The Smiths. *Wen hassen Tim und Tina? – Die Smiths.*
Who **hates** the Smiths? – Tim and Tina. *Wer hasst die Smiths? – Tim und Tina.*

Tina wakes Tim every morning. *Tina weckt Tim jeden Morgen.*
Who **does** Tina **wake**? – Tim. *Wen weckt Tina? – Tim.*
Who **wakes** Tim? – Tina. *Wer weckt Tim? – Tina.*

Tina phoned Tim at the office yesterday. *Tina rief Tim gestern im Büro an.*
Who **did** Tina **phone**? – Tim. *Wen hat Tina angerufen? – Tim.*
Who **phoned** Tim? – Tina. *Wer rief Tim an? – Tina.*

Entsprechend ist der Gebrauch in Fragen mit what.

1. Ergänzen Sie die Rückfrage mit did.

I phoned Elizabeth. – Sorry, who *did* you *phone*?

a We met Phil at the party. – Sorry, who ________ you ________?
b I visited David and Sarah last weekend. – Sorry, who ________ you ________?
c The police arrested an 80-year-old man. – Sorry, who ________ the police ________?
d We asked a priest the way. – Sorry, who ________ you ________ the way?
e Ann saw the Queen. – Sorry, ________ ________ Ann ________?
f I taught my mother to swim. – Sorry, ________ ________ you ________ to swim?

2. Bilden Sie eine Frage mit do oder does.

What / you / want? – We need some help with our car.
What do you want? – We need some help with our car.

a What / this / cost? ________ – It costs €35.
b What / you / think? ________ – I think it's a good idea.
c What / you / serve / with this fish? ________ – I usually serve white wine.
d What / people without a car / do? ________ – They take a taxi.
e What / you / do / at weekends? ________ – We often go to the mountains.
f What / say / the thermometer? ________ – Minus 8.

3. Wie lautet die who-Frage: mit did oder ohne did?

I asked XXXXX. ➡ *Who did you ask?* XXXXX phoned. ➡ *Who phoned?*

a We met XXXXX at the party. ➡ Who ________?
b XXXXX paid. ➡ Who ________?
c XXXXX arrived last, of course. ➡ ________ last?
d XXXXX planned the whole thing. ➡ ________?
e Ben says that XXXXX won. ➡ Who ________?
f Angela told me that she phoned XXXXX. ➡ ________?

4. Übersetzen Sie. (Die Verben stehen in der einfachen Gegenwart oder Vergangenheit.)

a Was willst du?
b Was kostet dieser Pullover?
c Wer hat gestern Abend angerufen?
d Wen kennst du hier?
e Was passiert in dem Film?
f Wen habt ihr auf der Party letztes Wochenende getroffen?

Who were you talking to?

Mit wem hast du gesprochen?

1 Lügner 2 Zeitansage

Who … to?

Tinas Frage Who were you talking to? heißt auf Deutsch „Mit wem hast du da gerade gesprochen?“. Uns interessiert in dieser Gegenüberstellung die Position des Fragewortes (who bzw. „wem“) und der Präposition (to bzw. „mit“). Im Deutschen steht die Präposition am Satzanfang vor dem Fragewort, im Englischen dagegen steht to am Satzende. Diese Satzstellung mag auf den ersten Blick ungewöhnlich wirken (wörtlich: „Wem hast du gesprochen mit?“), ist aber die im Englischen übliche.

Regel In Fragen mit Fragewörtern (who, what, where, which) steht eine Präposition (in, of, with, to usw.) normalerweise am Satzende, hinter dem Verb und dessen Ergänzungen.

Who were you talking **to**? *Mit wem hast du da gerade gesprochen?*
What are they looking **for**? *Wonach suchen sie?*
What are you so sad **about**? *Worüber bist du so traurig?*
Where did you fly **to**? *Wohin seid ihr geflogen?*
Which country does she come **from**? *Aus welchem Land kommt sie?*

Die Präposition steht also dort, wo sie auch in einem Aussagesatz stehen würde.

	He went on holiday	with	his parents.
Who did	he go on holiday	with?	
	They are looking	for	somewhere to park.
What	are they looking	for?	

1. Schreiben Sie die Fragen um. Stellen Sie die Präposition ans Satzende.

~~With~~ who do you usually go on holiday? ➡ *Who do you usually go on holiday with?*

a ~~For~~ who do you work? ➡ ______

b ~~In~~ what are you interested? ➡ ______

c ~~From~~ where do you come? ➡ ______

d ~~In~~ what do you believe? ➡ ______

e ~~In~~ which part of the country do you live? ➡ ______

f ~~At~~ what are you especially good? ➡ ______

2. Bilden Sie eine Frage mit did you . . . . Stellen Sie die Präposition ans Satzende.

We flew to XXXXX. ➡ *Where did you fly to?*

a We stayed in the XXXXX Hotel. ➡ Which hotel ______?

b We went sailing with XXXXX. ➡ Who ______?

c We drove around in a XXXXX. ➡ What ______?

d We sent postcards of the XXXXX. ➡ What ______?

e We looked for some XXXXX. ➡ What ______?

f We bought souvenirs for XXXXX. ➡ Who ______?

3. Bilden Sie eine Frage. Verwenden Sie die gleiche Zeitform wie in der Antwort.

to / who / you / give / the keys? – I gave them to Ann.

Who did you give the keys to? – I gave them to Ann.

a with / who / you / go on holiday?

______? – I'm going with friends.

b about / what / the boss / be / so angry?

______? – He was angry with me.

c of / what / you / be afraid?

______? – I was afraid that I couldn't do it.

d with / who / Tom / play / tennis yesterday?

______? – Jack, and Jack won.

e with / who / old Mrs Lacy / live?

______? – She lives with her eldest daughter.

4. Übersetzen Sie. Verwenden Sie die angegebene Präposition und die Verlaufsform der Gegenwart.

Welche CD hörst du [gerade]? *(to)* *Which CD are you listening to?*

a Mit wem spricht er? *(to)*

b Worüber reden sie? *(about)*

c Auf was warten Sie? *(for)*

d An wen schreibst du? *(to)*

e Welche Wohnung schauen sie sich heute an? *(at)*

37

It's beautiful, isn't it?

Es ist doch wunderschön, nicht wahr?

It's ..., isn't it?

In dieser Unit beschäftigen wir uns mit einer eigenartigen Konstruktion im Englischen: Auf eine Aussage (It is ...) folgt gleich eine Frage (isn't it?) – wie ein Echo.
Die Kurzfrage nennen wir Frageanhängsel oder Bestätigungsfrage. Damit sucht der Sprecher eine Bestätigung oder Zustimmung von seinem Gesprächspartner. Im Deutschen verwenden wir in gleicher Funktion „(doch ...) nicht wahr?", „nicht?", „oder?".

Regel

In Bestätigungsfragen greifen wir Person und Hilfsverb aus unserem Satz wieder auf.
Ein bejahtes Hilfsverb verneinen wir in der Bestätigungsfrage.
Ein verneintes Hilfsverb bejahen wir in der Bestätigungsfrage.
He is 31, **isn't he?** *Er ist 31, nicht wahr?* He isn't older, **is he?** *Er ist nicht älter, oder?*

Bejaht	Verneint	Verneint	Bejaht
We are late,	**aren't we?**	We aren't late,	**are we?**
Ann can swim,	**can't she?**	Ann can't swim,	**can she?**
You've eaten,	**haven't you?**	You haven't eaten,	**have you?**
Dave will be there,	**won't he?**	Dave won't be there,	**will he?**
_______	_______	Peter doesn't smoke,	**does he?**
_______	_______	They don't know,	**do they?**
_______	_______	Tony didn't phone,	**did he?**

Nicht immer ist ein Hilfsverb im Satz vorhanden. Wenn das Verb in der einfachen Gegenwart oder der Vergangenheit steht und nicht verneint ist, müssen wir in der Bestätigungsfrage doesn't, don't oder didn't einsetzen.

	Aussage	Bestätigungsfrage	
Einfache Gegenwart	Peter smokes,	**doesn't he?**	*Peter raucht, nicht wahr?*
	They know,	**don't they?**	*Sie wissen Bescheid, nicht wahr?*
Vergangenheit	Tony phoned,	**didn't he?**	*Tony rief an, nicht wahr?*

1. Kreuzen Sie die richtige Form an.

a Toby works for IBM, …?
- doesn't he
- isn't he

b Joanna isn't working at the moment, …?
- is she
- does she

c I'm not the last, …?
- am I
- are I

d You weren't here last week, …?
- was you
- were you

e They went to France, …?
- didn't they
- went they

f We've finished, …?
- aren't we
- haven't we

2. Ergänzen Sie die Bestätigungsfrage. Sie brauchen immer eine Form von be.

You're English, *aren't you?*

a You aren't American, ________________?
b I'm not disturbing you, ________________?
c The colours are beautiful, ________________?
d It's a lovely day, ________________?
e The tickets weren't very expensive, ________________?
f You're waiting to see Mrs Evans, ________________?

3. Ordnen Sie zu: does, don't, has, haven't, wasn't, will.

a It was a really interesting programme, ________________ it?
b Ellen doesn't eat meat, ________________ she?
c You've paid the bill, ________________ you?
d Jim hasn't written, ________________ he?
e It won't be cold there, ________________ it?
f We need more time, ________________ we?

4. Ergänzen Sie die Bestätigungsfrage. Sie brauchen immer eine Form von do.

a You speak Italian, ________________?
b This wine tastes wonderful, ________________?
c Your husband works at home, ________________?
d They know our address, ________________?
e Where's the car? We parked on floor 5, ________________?
f I gave you my phone number, ________________?

38 We won't be able to go.

Wir werden nicht hingehen können.

won't be able to …

Das Verb can (Verneinung: can't / cannot) hat zwar die Vergangenheitsform could (Verneinung: couldn't), aber keine Present-Perfect- oder Zukunftsform. Statt dessen muss man ein so genanntes Ersatzverb verwenden: be able to. In Tinas Hiobsbotschaft für Tim („Wir werden nicht hingehen können") steht die Zukunftsform won't be able to.

Regel can hat keine Present-Perfect- oder Zukunftsform. Diese Zeiten bilden wir mit dem Ersatzverb be able to.

	Bejaht	Verneint
Gegenwart	I **can** read Italian.	I **can't** speak it.
	Ich kann Italienisch lesen.	*Ich kann es nicht sprechen.*
Vergangenheit	Glenn **could** walk at 15 months.	He **couldn't** talk.
	Glenn konnte mit 15 Monaten laufen.	*Er konnte nicht sprechen.*
Present Perfect	I've **been able to** rest.	I **haven't been able to** sleep.
	Ich habe mich ausruhen können.	*Ich habe nicht schlafen können.*
Zukunft	We'll **be able to** come.	We **won't be able to** stay.
	Wir werden kommen können.	*Wir werden nicht bleiben können.*

! can (sowie could und be able to) gebrauchen wir nicht allein – wie es im Deutschen manchmal möglich ist.

Er kann Spanisch und Portugiesisch. = He can **speak** Spanish and Portuguese.

Kannst du's oder brauchst du Hilfe? = Can you **do** it, or do you need help?

1. Kreuzen Sie die richtige Form an.

a I … do it for you next Saturday.
- ☐ will can
- ☐ will be able to

b My secretary … a little Japanese.
- ☐ can
- ☐ can speak

c We … find anywhere to park. Everywhere was full.
- ☐ can't
- ☐ couldn't

d Have you … find somewhere to stay?
- ☐ be able to
- ☐ been able to

e When … be able to let me know?
- ☐ are you
- ☐ will you

f Tony can ski, but his son … better.
- ☐ can do it
- ☐ can it

2. Schreiben Sie auf ein Blatt Sätze über sich mit could und couldn't.

swim, play the piano, ski, play the guitar, play chess, ride a horse, speak English, surf, ride a bike, use a computer	at the age of 3 / 4 / 5 / … when I was a child

Beispiele: *I could swim at the age of 5. / I couldn't use a computer when I was a child.*

3. Bilden Sie Sätze mit der Present-Perfect- oder Zukunftsform von be able to.

a I ______________________ *(find)* the address. Here it is.

b Sorry, but we ______________________ *(not come)* to your party next week.

c The system is working again now at last, but we ______________________ *(not phone)* all day.

d When ______________________ *(you tell)* me? I need to know as soon as possible.

e I'm afraid I ______________________ *(not repair)* your bike yet. I haven't had time.

f ______________________ *(Tony help)* you? – No. He was here, but he couldn't find the fault.

4. Übersetzen Sie.

a Wir werden Ihnen nächste Woche Bescheid geben[1] können.

b Bernds Mutter ist Amerikanerin. Er kann zwei Sprachen, Deutsch und Englisch.

c Hast du mit deinen Eltern sprechen können?

d Wir konnten mehr als 100 Kilometer [weit][2] sehen.

e Ich kann kein Spanisch. Kannst du verstehen, was der Mann will?

f Ben wird kommen können, aber ich arbeite samstags.

[1] let … know [2] Wörter in eckigen Klammern müssen nicht übersetzt werden.

39 You don't have to come.

Du musst nicht mitkommen.

you don't have to …

Im Deutschen würde Tim wohl sagen: „Du musst nicht mitkommen." Damit würde er meinen: es ist nicht nötig, dass du mitkommst, du brauchst nicht mitzukommen.
Im Englischen steht aber auffallenderweise You don't have to come (und nicht: ~~You mustn't come~~). Hier haben wir es mit einer gemeinen Sprachfalle zu tun.

Regel must entspricht „müssen" und drückt einen Befehl aus.
must not entspricht „nicht dürfen" (nicht: „~~nicht müssen~~") und drückt ein Verbot aus.
You **must** do your homework first. *Du musst zuerst deine Hausaufgaben machen.*
You **must** keep your password secret. *Du musst dein Passwort geheim halten.*
You **mustn't** feed the animals. *Du darfst die Tiere nicht füttern.*
You **mustn't** tell anyone what I said. *Du darfst niemandem erzählen, was ich gesagt habe.*

Ein Verbot mit mustn't kann man auch gegenüber sich selbst aussprechen.
It's Tony's birthday tomorrow. I **mustn't** forget. *… Ich darf ihn nicht vergessen.*
We **mustn't** be late. *Wir dürfen nicht zu spät kommen.*

! „nicht müssen" wird durch don't / doesn't have to wiedergegeben. Damit drücken wir aus, dass etwas nicht nötig ist.
I can take a taxi. You **don't have to** drive me. *… Du musst mich nicht fahren.*
Tom **doesn't have to** work at weekends. *Tom muss am Wochenende nicht arbeiten.*

Anstelle von don't / doesn't have to können wir auch needn't verwenden.
You **don't have to** tell me if you don't want to.
You **needn't** tell me if you don't want to.
Du musst / brauchst es mir nicht (zu) sagen, wenn du nicht willst.

1. Ergänzen Sie don't have to oder doesn't have to.

a A pullover is enough. He ________________ wear a jacket.
b You ________________ do anything. Everything is organized.
c We ________________ pay now.
d The children ________________ come with us if they don't want to.
e We ________________ hurry. There's plenty of time.
f Wait and see. A documentary film ________________ be boring.

2. Korrigieren Sie. Verwenden Sie eine Form von have to.

a There are still lots of tickets. We ~~mustn't~~ book. ________________
b You ~~mustn't~~ be very athletic to play golf. ________________
c I know what to do. She ~~mustn't~~ ask Tim for help. ________________
d It's one of these 24-hour supermarkets. He ~~mustn't~~ go shopping now. ________________ He can go later.
e I'm lucky. I ~~mustn't~~ paint the flat when I move out. ________________
f We can stay at home if you want. We ~~mustn't~~ go out. ________________

3. Kreuzen Sie die richtige Form an.

a Peter, you … park here. These spaces are reserved for women.
☐ don't have to
☐ mustn't

b We … pack a picnic. We can buy something on the way.
☐ mustn't
☐ needn't

c It's Sunday tomorrow, so we … get up so early, thank goodness.
☐ don't have to
☐ mustn't

d Mark … come till later if he doesn't want to.
☐ mustn't
☐ needn't

e That was really stupid of me. I really … do it again.
☐ don't have to
☐ mustn't

f The Smiths are very informal, so those jeans you're wearing will be OK. You … change.
☐ mustn't
☐ needn't

4. Übersetzen Sie die deutschen Sätze.

a It's Edna's birthday tomorrow. *Ich darf ihn nicht vergessen.*
b We can watch TV. *Wir müssen nicht Musik hören.*
c It's OK, I can manage. *Du musst mir nicht helfen.*
d He's got a bike, hasn't he? *Er muss nicht [Auto][1] fahren.*
e I don't want anyone to know. *Sie dürfen [es][1] niemandem sagen.*
f Oysters and champagne is fine. *Es muss nicht immer Kaviar* (caviar) *sein.*

[1]Wörter in eckigen Klammern müssen nicht übersetzt werden.

40 You'll have to walk to ...

Du wirst bis zu ... laufen müssen.

you'll have to ...

Ob es gerecht ist, dass Tina fährt, Tim aber bis ins nächste Dorf laufen soll, sei dahingestellt. Uns interessiert hier die Aussage you'll have to walk (du wirst laufen müssen). Die Form ~~will must~~ gibt es nicht, denn must ist – wie can (→ Unit 38) – unvollständig; wir brauchen ein Ersatzverb für die Vergangenheits-, Present-Perfect- und Zukunftsform.

Regel must existiert nur als Gegenwartsform (mit der Verneinung mustn't → Unit 39). Die Zeitstufen Vergangenheit, Present Perfect und Zukunft bilden wir mit dem Ersatzverb have to.

Gegenwart	I **must** do more sport. *Ich muss mehr Sport treiben.*
Vergangenheit	They **had to** wait. *Sie mussten warten.*
Present Perfect	We've **had to** call the doctor. *Wir haben den Arzt rufen müssen.*
Zukunft	You'll **have to** pay extra. *Sie werden extra zahlen müssen.*

mustn't entspricht „nicht dürfen", „nicht müssen" wird mit don't / doesn't have to ausgedrückt (→ Unit 39). Das Hilfsverb do + have to kommt auch in Fragen zum Einsatz.

	Verneinung	Frage
Gegenwart	I **don't have to** get up early.	Do you **have to** get up early?
	Ich muss nicht früh aufstehen.	*Müssen Sie früh aufstehen?*
	Tony **doesn't have to** go.	**Does** Ben **have to** go?
	Tony muss nicht hingehen.	*Muss Ben hingehen?*
Vergangenheit	We **didn't have to** wait.	**Did** you **have to** wait?
	Wir mussten nicht warten.	*Musstet ihr warten?*

1. Kreuzen Sie die richtige Form an.

a I … go again. The doctor says everything is OK now.
- ☐ don't have to
- ☐ haven't to

b We … wait two hours. It was terrible.
- ☐ had to
- ☐ must

c When will you … get up?
- ☐ have to
- ☐ must

d Peter has lost his job. He … his car.
- ☐ has had to sell
- ☐ has had to sold

e … to pay cash?
- ☐ Do customers have
- ☐ Have customers

f I couldn't go to the party because I … work.
- ☐ had to
- ☐ must

2. Eine Urlaubsreise ist geplant. Bilden Sie Sätze mit We will have to … .

a *We'll have to pack the day before.*
b ______
c ______
d ______
e ______
f ______

Countdown for holiday
pack the day before
book a taxi
the evening before
go to bed early
get up at 4.30
leave home 5.15
have breakfast at airport

3. Ergänzen Sie eine Form von have to. Vergessen Sie das Hilfsverb do / does / did nicht.

I *don't have to go* *(not go)* yet, but I can't stay long.

a I ______ *(not pay)* for the children. They are free.
b If a customer doesn't like something, and takes it back, the shop ______ ______ *(not give)* the money back.
c We were lucky. We ______ *(not wait)* long.
d Why did he agree to lend them the money? He ______ *(not do)* it.
e When ______ *(you / start work)*? – At 7.30, but I finish at 2.30.
f How much ______ *(your friends / pay)*? – Only $55. That was cheap.
g What ______ *(he / do)*? – He had to do a written test and then there was an interview.
h ______ *(you / look)* for a long time before you found a hotel?

4. Übersetzen Sie mit have to.

a Die Passagiere mussten 90 Minuten warten.
b Du wirst einen Urlaubstag *(a day's holiday)* nehmen müssen.
c Musst du jedes Wochenende arbeiten? – Nein, nur zwei Wochenenden im Monat.
d Wann müssen wir bezahlen?
e Wann werden wir aufstehen müssen?
f Du wirst den Chef fragen müssen. Ich kann das nicht entscheiden.

May I introduce myself?

Darf ich mich vorstellen?

I … myself

Im Deutschen sagen wir „Darf ich mich vorstellen?". Im Englischen gibt es aber eine eigene Form, wenn wir „mich selbst" meinen: May I introduce myself (nicht: introduce ~~me~~).

Regel Im Rückbezug auf die gleiche Person verwenden wir im Englischen das *-self*-Reflexivpronomen. Im Singular endet das Pronomen auf -self. Im Plural endet es auf -selves.

I	myself	*ich*	*mich / mir*			we	ourselves	*wir*	*uns*	
you	yourself	*du*	*dich / dir;*	*Sie sich*		you	yourselves	*ihr*	*euch;*	*Sie sich*
he	himself	*er*	*sich*			they	themselves	*sie*	*sich*	
she	herself	*sie*	*sich*							
it	itself	*es*	*sich*							

I can see **myself** in the window. *Ich sehe mich im Fenster.*
Ann has hurt **herself**. *Ann hat sich verletzt.*
We didn't recognize **ourselves**. *Wir haben uns nicht wieder erkannt.*
I said to **myself**: now or never. *Ich sagte mir: jetzt oder nie.*
Why are you sending **yourself** a postcard? *Warum schickst du dir selber eine Postkarte?*

Das *-self*-Reflexivpronomen verwenden wir auch in der Bedeutung „selbst / selber".
He built the chair **himself**. *Er hat den Stuhl selbst gebaut.*
They designed the house **themselves**. *Sie haben das Haus selbst entworfen.*

1. Kreuzen Sie die richtige Form an.

a He says he has a gun so that he can protect … .
☐ him
☐ himself

b David told Ann, but she doesn't believe … .
☐ him
☐ himself

c You mustn't pay for … .
☐ me
☐ myself

d I want to pay for … .
☐ me
☐ myself

e I don't believe it! How can these people call … Christians?
☐ them
☐ themselves

f These symbols here on the side, what do people call …? – Icons.
☐ them
☐ themselves

2. Korrigieren Sie. Verwenden Sie -self/-selves.

a Have we got something that the children could do? They want to make ~~them~~ useful.
____

b We paid for ~~us~~. ______________________________

c Glenn didn't have a teacher. He taught ~~him~~ to swim. ______________________________

d Why work? This is a question I ask ~~me~~ all the time! ______________________________
____

e I don't like her. She only thinks about ~~her~~. ______________________________

f You two look great. Have you bought ~~you~~ new clothes? ______________________________
____

3. Ergänzen Sie das Pronomen.

a Anna, please make ______________ comfortable.

b I need a plaster. Tony has cut ______________ .

c It's time for us to get ______________ ready.

d When you've all made ______________ comfortable, I'll read you a story.

e Babies can't feed ______________ .

f I see ______________ as a butler or chauffeur in Monte Carlo.

4. Übersetzen Sie.

a Ich frage mich manchmal, warum er das tat.

b Sie bauten das Haus selbst.

c Darf ich mich vorstellen?

d Ich kann dir nicht helfen. Du musst dir selbst helfen.

e Er sagte sich: Das ist meine letzte Zigarette.

f Wir haben einen Verein *(club)* und nennen *(call)* uns "The Oldies".

He's fallen in love.

Er hat sich verliebt.

he's fallen in love

Tim hat sich also in sein neues Handy verliebt. Uns interessiert daran das Reflexivpronomen im Deutschen („sich verlieben"), aber dessen Fehlen im Englischen: dort heißt es einfach fall in love.

Regel Deutsche Reflexivverben entsprechen nicht immer Reflexivverben im Englischen.

Sie treffen sich jeden Montag. = They **meet** every Monday.

Das Wetter ändert sich. = The weather **is changing**.

Wir können uns nicht konzentrieren. = We can't **concentrate**.

Ich kann es mir nicht vorstellen. = I can't **imagine** it.

argue *sich streiten*	fall in love *sich verlieben*	lie down *sich hinlegen*
change *sich (ver)ändern / umziehen*	feel *sich fühlen*	meet *sich treffen (mit)*
complain *sich beschweren*	get divorced *sich scheiden lassen*	remember *sich erinnern*
concentrate *sich konzentrieren*	hurry *sich beeilen*	sit down *sich setzen*
decide *sich entscheiden*	imagine *sich vorstellen*	wonder *sich wundern / fragen*
		worry *sich Sorgen machen*

! each other

Im Deutschen können wir „sich" im Sinne von „einander", „sich gegenseitig" gebrauchen. Im Englischen verwenden wir in dieser Bedeutung kein Reflexivpronomen, sondern each other (oder one another).

They know **each other**. *Sie kennen sich [gegenseitig].*

We gave **each other** a mobile. *Wir haben uns gegenseitig ein Handy geschenkt.*

1. Kreuzen Sie die richtige Form an.

a Do you two know ...? Let me introduce you.
- ☐ each other
- ☐ yourselves

b Why can't you decide ...?
- ☐ –
- ☐ yourself

c We sat up all night telling ... our life-stories.
- ☐ each other
- ☐ us

d We ... again next Thursday.
- ☐ meet
- ☐ meet us

e Tony and I have known ... since we were children.
- ☐ each other
- ☐ us

f Our son says he can ... on his homework better if he has the radio on.
- ☐ concentrate
- ☐ concentrate himself

2. Wie übersetzt man hier „sich"?
– als herself, himself oder yourselves (→ Unit 41)?
– als each other?
– oder wird es gar nicht übersetzt?

a He looked at ________________ *(sich)* in the mirror.
b I don't think you two know ________________ *(sich)*. Let me introduce you.
c My mother always worries ________________ *(sich)* that something bad is going to happen.
d Come in and make ________________ *(sich)* comfortable. You can sit ________________ *(sich)* down here.
e What are you going to do? When are you going to decide ________________ *(sich)*?
f Is Ann OK? Did she hurt ________________ *(sich)*?

3. Übersetzen Sie.

a The service is awful. I'm going to ________________ *(mich beschweren)*.
b We really must ________________ *(uns treffen)* more often.
c Did you know? Carol and Jeremy have decided to ________________ *(sich scheiden lassen)*.
d I ________________ *(frage mich)* what he'll say. What do you think?
e We're going to be late. We must ________________ *(uns beeilen)*.
f I ________________ *(fühle mich)* great.

4. Übersetzen Sie.

a Wann war das? Kannst du dich erinnern?
b Wie fühlen Sie sich?
c Ich kann mich nicht konzentrieren.
d Unsere Welt hat sich verändert.
e Warum streitet ihr euch [gerade][1]?
f Unser Sohn hat sich wieder verliebt.

[1] Wörter in eckigen Klammern müssen nicht übersetzt werden.

43 Who is this woman who looks like you?

Wer ist diese Frau, die dir ähnlich sieht?

this woman who …

In Tims Frage steht zweimal who. Das erste who ist ein Fragepronomen und entspricht „wer" (Wer ist diese Frau?). Das zweite who ist ein Relativpronomen und entspricht „die" (die dir ähnlich sieht).

Mit einem Relativpronomen leiten wir einen Relativsatz ein. Mit einem Relativsatz bestimmen wir eine Person oder Sache näher und sagen, welche Person oder Sache wir genau meinen. Ein Relativsatz ist ein Satz im Satz. Das können wir uns so veranschaulichen:

Who is this woman?   The woman looks like you.

Satz 1   Satz 2

Who is this woman **who** looks like you? *Wer ist diese Frau, die dir ähnlich sieht?*

Regel

Relativsätze bestimmen Personen und Sachen näher.
Bei Personen verwenden wir who.
Bei Sachen verwenden wir which.

They have a daughter **who** is a model. *Sie haben eine Tochter, die Model ist.*

The man **who** wrote this is an expert. *Der Mann, der das geschrieben hat, ist ein Experte.*

Do you know the people **who** have bought number 77? *Kennst du die Leute, die Nr. 77 gekauft haben?*

A chef is someone **who** cooks in a restaurant or hotel. *Ein Chefkoch ist jemand, der in einem Restaurant oder Hotel kocht.*

There is one photo **which** shows the whole lake. *Es gibt ein Foto, das den ganzen See zeigt.*

It's the film **which** won all the Oscars. *Das ist der Film, der all die Oscars gewonnen hat.*

Anstelle von which können wir auch that verwenden.

I need something **that** will keep me warm. *Ich brauche etwas, das mich warm hält.*

that ist auch bei Personen möglich, who ist aber gebräuchlicher.

1. Kreuzen Sie die richtige Form an.

a Do you know the people … live next-door?
- ☐ they
- ☐ who

b I can't remember the name of the person … wrote it.
- ☐ which
- ☐ who

c I can't find a key … fits.
- ☐ that
- ☐ what

d He always does things … make me laugh.
- ☐ that
- ☐ they

e We've left the bag … has the map in it at home.
- ☐ who
- ☐ which

f He has an uncle … is a pilot.
- ☐ he
- ☐ who

2. Ergänzen Sie who oder which.

a I addressed it to "Angela, the girl ______________ drives the blue Golf, Exeter University".
b I don't like wearing clothes ______________ are too big.
c The people ______________ lived here before had cats.
d I'm going to take a photo of that house ______________ has graffiti all over it.
e I need to speak to someone ______________ understands English.
f She goes to a dentist ______________ uses hypnosis for narcosis.

3. Verbinden Sie die beiden Sätze zu einem.

A man showed us the way. He looked like a mafioso.
The man who showed us the way looked like a mafioso.

a A letter came this morning. It didn't have a stamp.
The letter ____

b A ball landed in our garden. It belonged to our neighbours' children.
The ball ____

c A woman took my name. She knows you.
The woman ____

d A car overtook us. It didn't have any lights.
The car ____

e A man came to the door. He said that he was a detective.
The man ____

f A girl served us. She was only about 13.
The girl ____

4. Übersetzen Sie.

a Sind Menschen, die rauchen, dünner?
b Ich mag Blumen, die riechen.
c Er ist jemand, der viel Schlaf braucht.
d Ein Millionär ist jemand, der viel Geld hat.
e Ich brauche eine Wohnung, die groß ist, aber nicht viel kostet.

... a recipe I found in a magazine.

... ein Rezept, das ich in einer Zeitschrift entdeckt habe.

It's a recipe I found ...

I found in a magazine ist ein Relativsatz (→ Unit 43) – allerdings ist das Relativpronomen which / that weggefallen. Das können wir uns so veranschaulichen:

It's a recipe. I found <u>the recipe</u> in a magazine.

It's a recipe (<u>which / that</u>) I found in a magazine.

Das Relativpronomen which / that stünde für the recipe: beide sind Objekt von found.

Regel Ist ein Relativpronomen Objekt im Relativsatz, so können wir es weglassen.
Wir erkennen, dass ein Relativpronomen Objekt ist, wenn zwischen Relativpronomen und Verb des Relativsatzes ein anderes Pronomen (z. B. I) oder ein Nomen (z. B. Tony) steht.

There's the man **(who / that)** I saw on the train this morning. [I saw <u>him</u> on the train ...]
Dort ist der Mann, den ich heute Morgen im Zug gesehen habe.

Ann Smith is the woman **(who / that)** Tony met on holiday. [Tony met <u>the woman</u> ...]
Ann Smith ist die Frau, die Tony im Urlaub kennen gelernt hat.

Where is the chocolate **(which / that)** I bought yesterday? [I bought <u>the chocolate</u> ...]
Wo ist die Schokolade, die ich gestern gekauft habe?

Die Präposition (with, at) in folgenden Relativsätzen steht dort, wo sie auch sonst in einem Aussagesatz stehen würde – hinter dem Verb (und dessen Ergänzungen). (→ Unit 36)

That is the woman. I saw Donald **with** <u>the woman</u> yesterday.
That is the woman (<u>who / that</u>) I saw Donald **with** yesterday.
Das ist die Frau, mit der ich Donald gestern gesehen habe.

How much is the model? You are looking **at** <u>the model</u> now.
How much is the model (<u>which / that</u>) you are looking **at** now?
Was kostet das Modell, das du dir jetzt gerade anschaust?

1. Kreuzen Sie den richtigen Satz an.

a ☐ What is the CD to that you are listening?
☐ What is the CD you are listening to?

b ☐ Dave is the person with who I played tennis last weekend.
☐ Dave is the person I played tennis with last weekend.

c ☐ We have some friends who moved to California last year.
☐ We have some friends moved to California last year.

d ☐ The rocks at that you are looking are some of the oldest in the world.
☐ The rocks you are looking at are some of the oldest in the world.

2. Ergänzen Sie who oder which – aber nur, wenn es unbedingt nötig ist.

a The book ________________ I read on holiday was fantastic.
b The plane ________________ crashed was over 30 years old.
c Do you know the name of the architect ________________ built this museum?
d Was the money ________________ I gave you enough?
e This is the jacket ________________ I bought in the winter sales.
f The customer ________________ complained got €50 back.

3. Verbinden Sie die beiden Sätze zu einem.

The bus never came. I was waiting for it.
The bus I was waiting for never came.

a Did you find the book? You were looking for it.
Did you find ____?

b This is the house. I lived in it as a child.
This is the house ____.

c Where is the magazine? I left it on the sofa.
Where is ____?

d Who was the woman? You were speaking to her.
Who was ____?

e Josie is a friend. I was at school with her.
Josie is a ____.

4. Übersetzen Sie. Verwenden Sie das Relativpronomen nur wenn nötig.

a Der Mann, von dem ich die Information habe, ist ein Experte.
b Meine Kollegin hat einen Hund, der singt.
c Die Menschen, die wir dort trafen, waren alle sehr arm.
d Ist das der Schlüssel, den du [gerade][1] suchst?
e Ich kenne die Frau nicht, mit *(to)* der John [gerade][1] spricht.
f Das Geschenk, das ich für meine Eltern habe, ist sehr groß.

[1]Wörter in eckigen Klammern müssen nicht übersetzt werden.

Units 26–44

Wählen Sie die richtige Form.

used to

1. We ... have a boat.
   a) ☐ use to
   b) ☐ used to

Vorvergangenheit

2. I looked out, but the rain ... .
   a) ☐ hadn't stopped
   b) ☐ hasn't stopped

Die Zukunft

3. David Willet phoned while you were out. He ... back tomorrow.
   a) ☐ is going to phone
   b) ☐ phones

4. Tony and Angela ... a party next weekend.
   a) ☐ are giving
   b) ☐ give

5. David ... borrow our tent for two weeks. Is that OK?
   a) ☐ wants to
   b) ☐ will

6. One moment, please. ... if she's in her office.
   a) ☐ I see
   b) ☐ I'll see

7. I'm sorry, but there ... be enough time to stop for lunch.
   a) ☐ doesn't
   b) ☐ won't

8. I think ... another glass of wine. Waiter!
   a) ☐ I have
   b) ☐ I'll have

9. I'm sure you ... it. There is lots to see and do there.
   a) ☐ enjoy
   b) ☐ will enjoy

10. I'm afraid we ... any more details before next week.
   a) ☐ don't know
   b) ☐ won't know

11. We ... a ten-minute break now.
   a) ☐ have
   b) ☐ 'll have

Das Passiv

12. The table ... yesterday.
   a) ☐ is reserved
   b) ☐ was reserved

13. Dollars ... everywhere, but almost everywhere.
   a) ☐ aren't accepted
   b) ☐ don't be accepted

14. Oh no! My bag ... .
   a) ☐ has been stolen
   b) ☐ is stolen

15. A new road ... . It will be ready next year.
   a) ☐ is being built
   b) ☐ is built

16. The poster was designed ... a friend.
   a) ☐ by
   b) ☐ from

17. It's a fantastic story. – ...
   a) ☐ By who was it written?
   b) ☐ Who was it written by?

Fragen

18. Who … in the flat above you?
    a) does live
    b) lives

19. Who … to speak to?
    a) do you want
    b) wants

20. … a few minutes ago on the phone?
    a) To who were you speaking
    b) Who were you speaking to

21. Anita works for a media company, …?
    a) doesn't she
    b) isn't she

Modalverben

22. I'm sorry, but I just … find the time.
    a) haven't been able to
    b) haven't can

23. It's a holiday here tomorrow, so I … go to work.
    a) don't have to
    b) mustn't

24. … use English a lot in your job?
    a) Do you have to
    b) Must you

-self-Pronomen

25. We must get … ready. We have to leave in ten minutes.
    a) ourselves
    b) us

26. When can we … again? Is next Tuesday OK for you?
    a) meet
    b) meet us

27. They know … . They are members of the same sports club.
    a) each other
    b) themselves

Relativsätze

28. They have a son … is a missionary.
    a) he
    b) who

29. I am someone … needs a lot of sleep.
    a) which
    b) who

30. What was that music …?
    a) you were listening to
    b) to that you were listening

Vergleichen Sie nun Ihre Lösungen mit dem Schlüssel auf S. 160. Wenn Sie Aufgaben nicht richtig gelöst haben, wiederholen Sie noch einmal die betreffende Unit. Diese Tabelle zeigt Ihnen, auf welche Unit sich die einzelnen Aufgaben beziehen.

Aufgabe	Unit	Aufgabe	Unit
1	26	16	34
2	27	17	34
3	28	18	35
4	29	19	35
5	30	20	36
6	30	21	37
7	30	22	38
8	31	23	39
9	31	24	40
10	31	25	41
11	31	26	42
12	32	27	42
13	32	28	43
14	33	29	43
15	33	30	44

45 He likes having his nephew here.

Er mag es, seinen Neffen zu Besuch zu haben.

likes ...ing

In unserem Cartoontext steht hinter like die -ing-Form having. Diese -ing-Form hat – trotz gleicher Form – nichts mit der Verlaufsform des Verbs zu tun, sondern ist eine Art Nomen.

Vergleichen Sie: I like books. Books are one of my hobbies.
I like reading (das Lesen). Reading (Das Lesen) is one of my hobbies.

Regel Auf bestimmte Verben folgt im Englischen eine -ing-Form als Objekt.

Verben des Mögens und Nicht-Mögens	Verben des Beginnens, Fortsetzens und Beendens	Sonstige Verben
like doing *gern tun*	begin doing *beginnen zu tun*	avoid doing *vermeiden zu tun*
love doing *liebend gern tun*	start doing *anfangen zu tun*	imagine doing *sich vorstellen zu tun*
enjoy doing *gern tun, es genießen zu tun*	carry on doing *weiter tun*	practise doing *üben zu tun*
prefer doing *lieber tun*	continue doing *weiter tun*	risk doing *riskieren zu tun*
(not) mind doing *etwas / nichts dagegen haben zu tun*	finish doing *zu Ende tun*	suggest doing *vorschlagen zu tun*
hate doing *hassen, ungern haben/tun*	give up doing *aufgeben, aufhören zu tun*	
	stop doing *aufhören zu tun*	

I **enjoy working** at home. *Ich arbeite gern zu Hause.*

We **don't mind paying** more if it is really good. *Wir haben nichts dagegen, mehr zu zahlen, wenn es wirklich gut ist.*

Would you **mind staying** at home this evening? *Hättest du etwas dagegen, heute Abend zu Hause zu bleiben?*

Can you **imagine living** in the country? *Kannst du dir vorstellen auf dem Land zu leben?*

Ann **suggested flying**. *Ann hat vorgeschlagen zu fliegen.*

1. Ergänzen Sie die -ing-Form und unterstreichen Sie das davor stehende Verb.

a I hate ________________ *(get)* up early.
b Do you mind ________________ *(wait)*?
c Tom gave up ________________ *(smoke)* last year.
d You risk ________________ *(make)* an enemy of her.
e I love ________________ *(swim)* in the sea.
f I must practise ________________ *(write)* e-mails in English.

2. Schreiben Sie Sätze über sich mit der -ing-Form.

(don't) like love (don't) enjoy don't mind hate	work at night / at the weekend / in the garden / … live in the town / country get up early wear jeans go on holiday with … / to … / in … eat in bed eat exotic food write letters cook …

Beispiele: *I like living in the country.*
I hate eating in bed.

a ________________
b ________________
c ________________
d ________________
e ________________
f ________________

3. Formulieren Sie höfliche Bitten mit Would you mind … ?

Please wait. *Would you mind waiting?*
a Please repeat that. ________________
b Please leave us alone. ________________
c Switch off your mobile phone, please. ________________
d Please move your bag. ________________
e Don't smoke. ________________ not ________________
f Don't park here. ________________ not ________________

4. Korrigieren Sie.

a Can you imagine ~~to be~~ rich? ________________
b I really enjoy ~~to listen~~ to her. ________________
c I tried to avoid ~~to look~~ at it. ________________
d We don't want to risk ~~to break~~ it. ________________
e Practise ~~to say~~ that in English. ________________
f I suggest ~~to wait~~ till prices fall again. ________________

I would love to know ...

Ich würde liebend gern wissen ...

would love / prefer to ...

„Ich würde es liebend gern wissen", meint Tina. „Ich würde es lieber nicht wissen", meint Tim. Im Englischen steht nach would love / would prefer ein Infinitiv (= Grundform des Verbs) mit to: to know.

Regel Auf like, love, prefer, hate kann eine -ing-Form folgen (→ Unit 45) – oder aber ein to-Infinitiv. Auf would like, would love, would prefer, would hate kann nur ein to-Infinitiv folgen.

I **like swimming / to swim** in the sea. *Ich schwimme gern im Meer.*
I **would like to swim** in a tropical lagoon. *Ich würde gern in einer tropischen Lagune schwimmen.*

Tom **loves cooking / to cook**. *Tom kocht liebend gern.*
Tom **would love to cook** in his own restaurant. *Tom würde liebend gern in seinem eigenen Restaurant kochen.*

Ann **prefers travelling / to travel** to work by train. *Ann fährt lieber mit dem Zug zur Arbeit.*
I **would prefer to travel** by car. *Ich würde lieber mit dem Auto fahren.*

Andy **hates working / to work** at night. *Andy arbeitet sehr ungern nachts.*
I **would hate to work** at night, too. *Ich würde auch sehr ungern nachts arbeiten.*

Auf viele andere Verben folgt – wie im Deutschen – nur ein to-Infinitiv.

afford *sich leisten*	manage *es schaffen*	refuse *sich weigern*
decide *sich entscheiden*	offer *anbieten*	seem *scheinen*
hope *hoffen*	plan *planen*	want *wollen*
learn *lernen*	promise *versprechen*	

I can't **afford to** go on holiday. *Ich kann es mir nicht leisten, in Urlaub zu fahren.*
We **decided to wait**. *Wir haben uns entschieden zu warten.*

1. Kreuzen Sie die richtige Form an.

a I like … a cold shower.
- ☐ have
- ☐ having

b I would hate … that happen.
- ☐ seeing
- ☐ to see

c Would you prefer … in the evening?
- ☐ eating
- ☐ to eat

d What have you decided …?
- ☐ doing
- ☐ to do

e Thank you. We'd love … .
- ☐ coming
- ☐ to come

f What are you planning … next?
- ☐ doing
- ☐ to do

2. Bilden Sie Fragen mit … would you like / prefer to …?

(when / like / get up) *When would you like to get up?*
(prefer / eat / now or later) *Would you prefer to eat now or later?*
a (where / like / go / today) ____________________
b (prefer / stay / at home this evening) ____________________
c (what / like / see) ____________________
d (which programme / prefer / watch) ____________________
e (like / try / a piece of Christmas Cake) ____________________
f (what / prefer / do / today) ____________________

3. Kreuzen Sie alle möglichen Formen für folgenden Satz an.

I … in the afternoon.

	sleeping	to sleep
would love	☐	☐
want	☐	☐
always avoid	☐	☐
suggested	☐	☐
enjoy	☐	☐
hate	☐	☐
prefer not	☐	☐
have given up	☐	☐

	sleeping	to sleep
have stopped	☐	☐
never like	☐	☐
managed	☐	☐
decided	☐	☐
hoped	☐	☐
love	☐	☐
planned	☐	☐
would like	☐	☐

4. Übersetzen Sie.

a Tim hat angeboten zu helfen.
b Ich würde liebend gern Neuseeland besuchen.
c Kannst du dir vorstellen in Neuseeland zu wohnen?
d Ich schlage vor ein Taxi zu nehmen.
e Wir würden sehr ungern mehr bezahlen.
f Es hat aufgehört zu regnen. Wir können gehen.

47 We're looking forward to seeing you, Mum.

Wir freuen uns darauf, dich zu sehen, Mama.

look forward to ...ing

Uns interessiert hier weniger Tims Verhältnis zu seiner Schwiegermama als Tinas Höflichkeitsfloskel und die -ing-Form seeing. Warum heißt es ... to seeing und nicht ... to see? Weil to Teil der festen Wendung look forward to (= sich freuen auf) ist. Auf diese Wendung kann ein Nomen folgen – oder ein Verb.

We're looking forward to your visit.
(= Wir freuen uns auf deinen Besuch.)

We're looking forward to seeing you.
(= Wir freuen uns darauf, dich zu sehen.)

Regel Nach einer Präposition steht ein Verb immer in der -ing-Form, nicht im Infinitiv.
Präpositionen sind Wörter wie: about, against, at, for, from, in, like, of, on, to, with, worth.
Eine Präposition ist oft Teil einer Wendung, die aus Verb + Präposition besteht.

We have often thought about **moving**. *Wir haben oft daran gedacht umzuziehen.*
Is it worth **waiting** for Jack? *Lohnt es sich, auf Jack zu warten?*
Do you feel like **seeing** a film this evening? *Hast du Lust heute Abend einen Film anzuschauen?*
I have often dreamed of **opening** a restaurant. *Ich habe oft davon geträumt, ein Restaurant zu eröffnen.*
We are used to **getting up** (~~to get up~~) early. *Wir sind daran gewöhnt, früh aufzustehen.*

apologize for doing sth *sich dafür entschuldigen, etwas zu tun*
be against doing sth *dagegen sein etwas zu tun*
be used to doing sth *gewöhnt sein etwas zu tun*
be worth doing sth *sich lohnen etwas zu tun*
concentrate on doing sth *sich darauf konzentrieren, etwas zu tun*
dream of / about doing sth *davon träumen, etwas zu tun*
feel like doing sth *Lust haben etwas zu tun*
look forward to doing sth *sich darauf freuen, etwas zu tun*
speak about doing sth *davon sprechen, etwas zu tun*
talk about doing sth *davon sprechen, etwas zu tun*
thank sb for doing sth *jemandem dafür danken, dass er etwas tut*
think about / of doing sth *daran denken, etwas zu tun*
worry about doing sth *sich Sorgen machen etwas zu tun*

1. Ergänzen Sie die -ing-Form und unterstreichen Sie die davor stehenden Verben mit Präpositionen.

Are you looking forward to <u>*seeing*</u> *(see)* them?

a Have you ever thought of ________________ *(start)* your own business?
b Do you feel like ________________ *(come)* with me?
c I'm not used to ________________ *(cook)* for so many people.
d We're thinking of ________________ *(buy)* a new car.
e Tony apologized for ________________ *(wake)* me up.
f We are all against ________________ *(invite)* our boss to the party.

2. Korrigieren Sie.

a People here are used to ~~drive~~ long distances to work.
____

b I am really looking forward to ~~finish~~ this project.
____

c No more, thanks. I'm not used to ~~drink~~ so much.
____

d Andy is looking forward to ~~surf~~ again in the summer.
____

3. Ergänzen Sie die richtige Präposition und die -ing-Form.

a I apologize ________________ ________________ *(be)* so late.
b They are concentrating first ________________ ________________ *(repair)* the bridge.
c They thanked me ________________ ________________ *(look)* after their cat.
d Do you ever dream ________________ ________________ *(be)* a millionaire?
e I feel ________________ ________________ *(have)* a nice hot bath.
f Don't worry ________________ ________________ *(make)* mistakes. Just talk.

4. Übersetzen Sie.

a Wir haben immer davon geträumt, Tibet zu besuchen.
b Es lohnt sich nicht zu warten.
c Hast du Lust, einen Film zu sehen?
d Haben Sie je daran gedacht, eine Wohnung zu kaufen?
e Ich freue mich darauf, in Urlaub zu fahren.
f Mein Sohn ist nicht gewohnt hart zu arbeiten.

48 I'm not good at remembering names.

Ich kann mir Namen nicht gut merken.

good at ...-ing

Aus Unit 47 wissen wir, dass nach einer Präposition (hier: at) ein Verb immer in der -ing-Form steht (hier: remembering). In dieser Unit beschäftigen wir uns mit eher idiomatischen Wendungen mit Präposition, auf die ein Verb in der -ing-Form folgt.

Regel Nach einer Präposition folgt ein Verb in der -ing-Form, nicht im Infinitiv!

I am good / bad at **remembering** names. *Ich kann mir Namen gut / schlecht merken.*

She is afraid of **being** late. *Sie hat Angst zu spät zu kommen.*

He was tired of **waiting** / was fed up with **waiting** and went home. *Er hatte das Warten satt und ging nach Hause.*

She was excited about **going** to America. *Sie freute sich darauf, nach Amerika zu fahren.*

Are you interested in **finding** out more? *Sind Sie daran interessiert, mehr zu erfahren?*

Edison is famous for **inventing** the electric light bulb. *Edison ist berühmt dafür, dass er die Glühbirne erfunden hat.*

I like the idea / thought of **working** from home. *Mir gefällt die Idee / der Gedanke von zu Hause aus zu arbeiten.*

He had the habit of **writing** / He was in the habit of **writing** angry letters. *Er hatte die Angewohnheit zornige Briefe zu schreiben.*

What are the chances of **finding** a hotel? *Wie stehen die Chancen ein Hotel zu finden?*

We had the choice of **walking** home or **getting** a taxi. *Wir hatten die Wahl nach Hause zu laufen oder ein Taxi zu rufen.*

What was your reason for **doing** this? *Was war der Grund, dass Sie das getan haben?*

We are in danger of **losing** touch. *Wir laufen Gefahr den Kontakt zu verlieren.*

I had difficulty in **opening** the window. *Ich hatte Schwierigkeiten das Fenster zu öffnen.*

We are in the process of **modernizing** our kitchen. *Wir sind dabei, unsere Küche zu modernisieren.*

Is there an alternative to **going** by car? *Gibt es eine Alternative dazu, mit dem Auto zu fahren?*

1. Ergänzen Sie die -ing-Form und unterstreichen Sie den davor stehenden Ausdruck.

a Are you interested in ________________ *(come)* with me?
b They have developed a new method of ________________ *(grow)* tomatoes.
c Caroline is in the habit of ________________ *(forget)* people's names.
d We were afraid of ________________ *(wake)* you up.
e Our team is in danger of ________________ *(lose)* the match.
f I am fed up with ________________ *(listen)* to his old jokes.

2. Korrigieren Sie.

a I hate the idea ~~to lose~~ an old friend.
____
b Do we have an alternative ~~to accept~~ this offer?
____
c My grandfather had the habit ~~to smoke~~ Havana cigars in the bath.
____
d We have the choice ~~to pay~~ now or later.
____
e The thought ~~to swim~~ in the sea every day is wonderful.
____
f I'm not interested ~~to play~~ chess.
____

3. Ergänzen Sie die richtige Präposition und die -ing-Form.

a Some people are very bad ________________ ________________ *(draw)*.
b I'm always afraid ________________ ________________ *(fall)* and ________________ *(break)* my leg.
c I cannot understand Daniel's reasons ________________ ________________ *(leave)* her.
d We were tired ________________ ________________ *(go)* to the same place every year.
e My son is really excited ________________ ________________ *(meet)* his favourite singer.
f Astrid Lindgren was famous ________________ ________________ *(write)* children's books.

4. Übersetzen Sie.

a Ich habe einen besonderen Grund David Waters einzuladen.
b Du läufst Gefahr den letzten Zug zu verpassen.
c David ist so schlecht im Planen.
d Wir hatten es satt, die gleichen Leute zu treffen.
e Ich bin nicht daran interessiert, Michael Schumacher zu treffen.
f Sie hat die Angewohnheit mitten in der Nacht anzurufen.

Instead of laughing, help me!

Anstatt zu lachen, hilf mir doch!

Instead of ...-ing

Aus den Units 47–48 wissen wir, dass nach einer Präposition ein Verb immer in der -ing-Form steht. Dort haben wir die -ing-Form mit Ausdrücken geübt, bei denen die Präposition mit einem Verb, Adjektiv oder Nomen eine feste Wendung einging (Konstruktion: Verb / Adjektiv / Nomen + Präposition + -ing-Form). Es gibt aber einige wenige (aber wichtige) Präpositionen, die allein stehen, d. h. keine feste Wendung mit einem vorausgehenden Wort bilden. In dieser Unit geht es um diese kleine Gruppe von Präpositionen.

Regel Direkt nach before, after, by, instead of, without steht ein Verb in der -ing-Form.

I always have a shower **before going** to bed. *Ich dusche immer, bevor ich ins Bett gehe.*

After watching the news, I went out to the pub. *Nachdem ich die Nachrichten angesehen hatte, bin ich in die Kneipe gegangen.*

You won't find any new friends **by staying** at home. *Du wirst keine neuen Freunde finden, indem du zu Hause bleibst.*

I phoned **instead of sending** an e-mail. *Ich habe angerufen, anstatt eine E-Mail zu schicken.*

She left **without giving** me a kiss. *Sie ist gegangen, ohne mir einen Kuss zu geben.*

Auch nach how about? und what about? steht ein Verb in der -ing-Form. Diese Wendungen verwenden wir, um einen Vorschlag zu machen.

How about going to the movies this evening? *Wir wäre es, wenn wir heute Abend ins Kino gehen?*

What about asking Thomas? He might know. *Wie wäre es, wenn wir Thomas fragen? Er könnte es wissen.*

1. Ergänzen Sie die -ing-Form und unterstreichen Sie die davor stehende Präposition.

a Check all the windows before ________________ *(leave)* the house.
b Wait 3–4 minutes after ________________ *(make)* the tea before ________________ *(drink)* it.
c I found out the address by ________________ *(ask)* a friend.
d Instead of ________________ *(sit)* there, why can't you help me?
e Please don't go out without ________________ *(tell)* me.

2. Machen Sie einen Vorschlag mit how about? oder what about?

It's a lovely day. – *(go to the sea)* How / What about going to the sea?
a We need some help. – *(ask Phil)* ________________
b I feel so tired. – *(go to bed early)* ________________
c I don't feel like cooking this evening. – *(eat out at that new restaurant)*
____
d What are we going to give Alice for her birthday? – *(buy her a CD)*
____
e What shall we do today? – *(take a boat on the river)*
____
f Would Angela know the address? – *(phone and ask her)*
____

3. Verbinden Sie die beiden Sätze zu einem, wie im Beispiel.

Read through all the test questions. Then start to answer them. *(before)*
Read through all the test questions before starting to answer them.
a Do something. Don't just sit there. *(instead of)* ________________
b I said it. I didn't think. *(without)* ________________
c John sent an e-mail. Then he went offline. *(before)*
____
d You can find out what Ann would like for her birthday. Ask Tony. *(by)*
____
e I always do exercises in bed. Then I get up. *(before)*
____
f You can save a lot of money. Check prices on the internet. *(by)*
____

4. Übersetzen Sie.

a Anstatt auf Tim zu warten, lasst uns Desmond fragen.
b Der Mann verließ das Restaurant ohne zu zahlen.
c Du öffnest die Mail, indem du hier klickst.
d Tony lernte Spanisch, indem er spanische Comics las.
e Wie wäre es, wenn wir heute Abend zu Hause bleiben?

50 I don't want him to know.

Ich will nicht, dass er es weiß.

I don't want him to know

Dass auf want ein to-Infinitiv folgt, wissen wir, und dass want to do something eine deutsche Entsprechung mit Infinitiv hat („etwas tun wollen"). In unserem Cartoontext aber folgt auf want zunächst eine Person (him / her) und dann erst der to-Infinitiv. Die entsprechende Konstruktion im Deutschen ist ganz anders, nämlich mit „dass". Vergleichen Sie:

I don't want to know. = Ich will es nicht wissen.

I don't want him to know. = Ich will nicht, dass er es weiß.

Regel Auf want und would like kann im Englischen kein that-Satz folgen! Statt dessen verwenden wir die Konstruktion want / would like + Objekt + to-Infinitiv.

Make yourselves comfortable. I want you to feel at home. *Macht es euch bequem. Ich will, dass ihr euch wie zu Hause fühlt.*

Do you want me to shut the window? *Willst du, dass ich das Fenster schließe?*

I would like you to meet Nick Bailey. *Ich möchte, dass Sie Nick Bailey kennen lernen.*

Would you like me to help? *Möchtest du, dass ich helfe?*

Bei vielen anderen Verben hat die Konstruktion Verb + Objekt + Infinitiv eine direkte Entsprechung im Deutschen.

Ask him to come in. *Bitte ihn hereinzukommen.*

We invited them to stay the night with us. *Wir haben sie eingeladen bei uns zu übernachten.*

ask sb to do sth *jn bitten etwas zu tun*	invite sb to do sth *jn einladen etwas zu tun*
advise sb to do sth *jm raten etwas zu tun*	order sb to do sth *jm befehlen etwas zu tun*
allow sb to do sth *jm erlauben etwas zu tun*	teach sb to do sth *jm beibringen etwas zu tun*
help sb to do sth *jm helfen etwas zu tun*	

1. Verteilen Sie die Aufgaben. Schreiben Sie Sätze mit I want.

(Toby) I want Toby to arrange my flights.

a *(Joe)* ______

b *(Lisa)* ______

c *(Peter)* ______

d *(Ann)* ______

e *(Doris)* ______

f *(William)* ______

arrange my flights – Toby
phone New York – Joe
do the photocopying – Lisa
make some coffee – Peter
send a fax to Chicago – Ann
book a table for lunch – Doris
book a hotel for me – William

2. Korrigieren Sie.

a I want ~~that you go~~ now.

______

b We would like ~~that you stay~~ the night.

______

c Would you like ~~that I help~~ with those bags?

______

d The boss wants ~~that someone works~~ this weekend.

______

e My partner would like ~~that we get~~ married.

______

f They don't want ~~that we pay~~ now. We can pay later.

______

3. Formulieren Sie um wie im Beispiel.

"Please come in." *(ask)* They asked me to come in.

a "Take warm clothes." *(advise)* My aunt ______

b "You may take photos." *(allow)* They ______

c "Stay and have dinner." *(invite)* They ______

d "Surfing is easy. I'll show you." *(teach)* Ann's friend ______

e "Please wait in the foyer." *(ask)* She ______

f "Install the program? I'll do that for you." *(help)* My friend ______

______

4. Übersetzen Sie.

a Ich will, dass du mir hilfst.

b Wir wollen nicht, dass die Kinder es hören.

c Möchten Sie, dass ich den Text übersetze?

d Ich will, dass du auf mich wartest.

e Möchten Sie, dass ich Kaffee koche *(make)*?

f Wir möchten, dass Sie mit uns nach London kommen.

I warned you not to park here.

Ich habe dich davor gewarnt, hier zu parken.

I warned you not to …

Im Deutschen enthält das Wort „warnen“ bereits den Gedanken „nicht“. Im Englischen muss es extra dazugesagt werden:

I warned you not to park here. = Ich habe dich davor gewarnt, hier zu parken.

In dieser Unit geht es um einige Besonderheiten der Konstruktion, die wir in Unit 50 kennen gelernt haben: Verb + Objekt + Infinitiv. Es geht um die Verben warn, tell, let und make.

Regel Wenn wir sagen, was jemand nicht tun soll, verwenden wir warn sb not to do sth oder tell sb not to do sth.

I warned you **not to buy** that old car. *Ich habe dich davor gewarnt, dieses alte Auto zu kaufen.*

We told them **not to wait**. *Wir haben ihnen gesagt, dass sie nicht warten sollen.*

tell sb to do sth entspricht „jm sagen, dass er etwas tun soll“. Beachten Sie, dass man nicht say in dieser Konstruktion benutzt!

I told (~~said~~) Peter **to phone back** later. *Ich habe Peter gesagt, dass er später zurückrufen soll.*

Tell (~~Say~~) them **to hurry** or we'll be late. *Sag ihnen, dass sie sich beeilen sollen, sonst kommen wir zu spät.*

let und make (beide „lassen“) verwenden wir mit einem Infinitiv ohne to.

Let me **come** with you. *Lass mich mitkommen. [lassen = zulassen, erlauben]*

They made me **wait** six hours. *Sie ließen mich sechs Stunden warten. [lassen = zwingen]*

1. Kreuzen Sie die richtige Form an.

a Ann let me … her mobile phone.
- ☐ to use
- ☐ use

b I told you … more than 150 euros.
- ☐ not to pay
- ☐ that you not pay

c The teacher made all the children … .
- ☐ stand up
- ☐ to stand up

d The guide warned them … in the snowstorm.
- ☐ not to go out
- ☐ to go out

e Please tell him … me at about 6 o'clock.
- ☐ expect
- ☐ to expect

f She … me to be careful because of thieves.
- ☐ said
- ☐ told

2. Korrigieren Sie.

a The teacher ~~said~~ the children to be quiet.

____

b Will you ~~say~~ Ben to make some extra copies, please?

____

c The doctor ~~said~~ me to give up smoking.

____

d Can you ~~say~~ Ann to phone home, please?

____

e We warn tourists ~~to take~~ too much cash with them.

____

f I warned you ~~to go~~ swimming so soon after that big lunch.

____

3. let oder make? Ergänzen Sie das Verb in der richtigen Zeitform.

a My parents ______________ *(ließen)* me stay up late on Saturday evenings.
b My mother ______________ *(ließ)* me wash my hands before every meal.
c I'll ______________ *(lassen)* you borrow my camera if you want.
d I'll ______________ *(lassen)* you pay for it if you break it.
e The police ______________ *(ließen)* the man answer a lot of questions.
f The police ______________ *(ließen)* the man go.

4. Übersetzen Sie.

a Ich habe dich davor gewarnt, zu viel von dem Wein zu trinken.
b Ich werde dich nicht gehen lassen, bis du dich entschuldigst *(apologize)*.
c Mein Kollege sagte mir, dass ich den Chef nicht stören *(disturb)* sollte.
d Ich werde dich nicht bezahlen lassen. Du bist heute mein Gast.
e Sag deinem Freund, dass er hereinkommen soll.
f Er ließ seine Sekretärin bis 10 Uhr abends arbeiten.

Units 45–51

Wählen Sie die richtige Form.

-ing-Form und Infinitiv

1. I enjoy … new people.
   a) ☐ meeting
   b) ☐ to meet

2. I'm sorry, I forgot … you that I would be late.
   a) ☐ telling
   b) ☐ to tell

3. We hope … you again soon.
   a) ☐ seeing
   b) ☐ to see

4. Do you mind …? I won't be more than two or three minutes.
   a) ☐ to wait
   b) ☐ waiting

5. I can't imagine … in a place where it's always hot.
   a) ☐ living
   b) ☐ to live

6. Have you managed … Ben?
   a) ☐ contacting
   b) ☐ to contact

7. They suggest … to the theatre together. What do you think?
   a) ☐ going
   b) ☐ to go

8. We can't afford … a new car.
   a) ☐ buying
   b) ☐ to buy

9. We plan … at about 8 o'clock.
   a) ☐ arriving
   b) ☐ to arrive

10. I would love … that film again. It was so good.
    a) ☐ seeing
    b) ☐ to see

11. Ann offered …, but I said we were OK.
    a) ☐ helping
    b) ☐ to help

12. We're looking forward to … you all again.
    a) ☐ see
    b) ☐ seeing

13. Would you like … some of the photos we took?
    a) ☐ seeing
    b) ☐ to see

14. I'm not used to … French any more. I've forgotten it all.
    a) ☐ speak
    b) ☐ speaking

15. What do you feel like … this evening?
    a) ☐ do
    b) ☐ doing

16. We are concentrating … the downstairs rooms first.
    a) ☐ on renovating
    b) ☐ to renovate

17. I'm against … experiments with animals.
    a) ☐ doing
    b) ☐ to do

18. He left without ... goodbye.
 a) ☐ saying
 b) ☐ to say

19. We're going to that new bistro. ... with us?
 a) ☐ How about coming
 b) ☐ Why not to come

20. I'm not very ... names.
 a) ☐ good at remembering
 b) ☐ good in remembering

21. Instead of ... there, you could help your mother in the kitchen.
 a) ☐ sitting
 b) ☐ to sit

22. What was their reason ... the shop? It was doing well, wasn't it?
 a) ☐ for selling
 b) ☐ sell

23. I hate the idea ... you. You have been a wonderful friend.
 a) ☐ of losing
 b) ☐ to lose

24. He's not interested ... girls yet. He's only 10.
 a) ☐ in meeting
 b) ☐ to meet

25. It's worth ... prices.
 a) ☐ comparing
 b) ☐ to compare

26. I want ... home by 11.30, is that clear?
 a) ☐ that you are
 b) ☐ you to be

27. Emma would like ... a course, but I don't want to.
 a) ☐ me to do
 b) ☐ that I do

28. I warned you ... Phil. He can't keep a secret.
 a) ☐ not to tell
 b) ☐ to tell

29. Let me ... that for you.
 a) ☐ do
 b) ☐ to do

30. The letter makes me ... every time I read it.
 a) ☐ laugh
 b) ☐ to laugh

Vergleichen Sie nun Ihre Lösungen mit dem Schlüssel auf S. 162. Wenn Sie Aufgaben nicht richtig gelöst haben, wiederholen Sie noch einmal die betreffende Unit. Diese Tabelle zeigt Ihnen, auf welche Unit sich die einzelnen Aufgaben beziehen.

Aufgabe	Unit	Aufgabe	Unit
1	45	16	47
2	46	17	47
3	46	18	49
4	45	19	49
5	45	20	48
6	46	21	49
7	45	22	48
8	46	23	48
9	46	24	48
10	46	25	47
11	46	26	50
12	47	27	50
13	46	28	51
14	47	29	51
15	47	30	51

52 You said that you knew the way.

Du sagtest, dass du den Weg wüsstest.

You said that you knew ...

Tim wird wörtlich gesagt haben: "I know the way" („Ich weiß den Weg"). Tina hätte diese Aussage direkt als Zitat wiedergeben können: You said, "I know the way" (Du sagtest: „Ich weiß den Weg"). Sie gibt jedoch Tims Äußerung indirekt wieder. Vergleichen Sie:

Tim sagte:		"I know the way."
Tina berichtet direkt:	You said,	"I know the way".
Tina berichtet indirekt:	You said that	you knew the way.

Regel In der indirekten Rede geben wir eine Äußerung mit Veränderungen wieder:

1. Wir leiten die indirekte Rede mit einem Verb des Berichtens ein, z. B. said.
2. Nach said folgt that oder auch unmittelbar der Bericht, ohne that.
3. Wir verändern die Person, z. B. I ➡ you.
4. Wir verändern die Zeitform des Verbs, z. B. know (Gegenwart) ➡ knew (Vergangenheit).

Achtung: nach said steht kein Komma (auch nicht vor that)![1]

Tom: "I'**m** ill." ➡ Tom <u>said</u> (that) he **was** ill.
Dave: "It'**s** very late." ➡ Dave <u>said</u> (that) it **was** very late.
Tourists: "We'**re** from Japan." ➡ The tourists <u>said</u> (that) they **were** from Japan.
Ann: "I **have** 30 euros." ➡ Ann <u>said</u> (that) she **had** 30 euros.
Sonia: "My cats **drink** tea." ➡ Sonia <u>said</u> (that) her cats **drank** tea.
Man: "The hotel **isn't** far." ➡ The man <u>said</u> (that) the hotel **wasn't** far.

Auch in verneinten Sätzen mit don't und doesn't verändern wir die Zeitform (zu didn't).

Boy: "I **don't like** school." ➡ The boy <u>said</u> (that) he **didn't like** school.
Patient: "It **doesn't hurt**." ➡ The patient <u>said</u> (that) it **didn't hurt**.

[1]Bei der direkten Rede steht zwischen said und den Anführungszeichen ein Komma – kein Doppelpunkt wie im Deutschen. Die Anführungszeichen stehen immer oben: He said, "I know."

1. Setzen Sie, wo nötig, Komma und Anführungszeichen ein.

a Our neighbours said their house was too small.
b Tim said that he knew the way.
c Tina said It's time to get up.
d The ticket collector said Tickets please.
e My boss said What a terrible day!
f Our son said that he wanted to leave school.

2. Setzen Sie in die indirekte Rede.

Americans: "We aren't from Chicago."
➡ The Americans said _they weren't from Chicago_.
a Ann: "I feel cold." ➡ Ann said ______
b Toby: "We're too early." ➡ Toby said ______
c Peter: "I need more time." ➡ Peter said ______
d Boss: "The situation doesn't look good."
➡ The boss said ______
e Passenger: "I hate travelling at night."
➡ The passenger said ______
f Son: "I'm not ready." ➡ My son said ______
g Teacher: "I don't know the answer."
➡ The teacher said ______
h Man: "I don't speak German." ➡ The man said ______

3. Erwidern Sie wie im Beispiel.

"Sorry, I don't want anything." *(be hungry)* – _But you said you were hungry._
a "I don't want anything to drink." *(be thirsty)* – But you said ______
b "Sorry, I'm too tired." *(want to go out)* – But ______
c "I can't do it." *(it be easy)* – But ______
d "We can't buy it. It costs too much." *(it be cheap)* – But ______
e "We can't get in." *(have a key)* – But ______
f "I'm not going swimming." *(the water be nice and warm)* – But ______
______

4. Übersetzen Sie. Verwenden Sie bei den Verben die Vergangenheitsform.

a Mein Mann sagte, Whisky sei besser als Wein.
b Der Chef sagte, ich sei für die Stelle überqualifiziert *(overqualified)*.
c Aber du sagtest, du würdest kurze Haare mögen.
d Meine Tochter sagte, dass sie nicht mit uns in Urlaub fahren wolle.
e Tony sagte, der Hund beiße nicht.
f Meine Freunde sagten, ich sähe wie ein Gespenst *(ghost)* aus.

I said that I was meeting a friend.

Ich sagte doch, dass ich einen Freund treffen würde.

I said that I was meeting …

Tim wird wörtlich gesagt haben: "I am meeting a friend this evening" („Ich treffe heute Abend einen Freund"). In der indirekten Rede wird I'm meeting (Verlaufsform der Gegenwart) zu I was meeting (Verlaufsform der Vergangenheit). Aus Unit 52 kennen wir das Prinzip der Zeitverschiebung in der indirekten Rede (dort: Gegenwart ➡ Vergangenheit). In dieser Unit üben wir die Zeitverschiebung mit anderen Zeiten.

Regel In der indirekten Rede geben wir eine Äußerung mit Zeitverschiebung wieder.

Verlaufsform der Gegenwart	➡	Verlaufsform der Vergangenheit
"We're **having** our supper."	➡	Sheila said they **were having** their supper.
"You **aren't working** very hard."	➡	The boss said we **weren't working** very hard.
Present Perfect	➡	Past Perfect
"Ann **has won** first prize."	➡	Brian said that Ann **had won** first prize.
"I **haven't seen** Sonia."	➡	Roger said he **hadn't seen** Sonia.
can	➡	could
"I **can** speak Spanish."	➡	Tim said he **could** speak Spanish.
"I **can't** swim."	➡	Donald said that he **couldn't** swim.
will	➡	would
"I'**ll** call back."	➡	The woman said she **would** call back.
"I **won't** tell you again."	➡	His mother said she **wouldn't** tell him again.

Eine Vergangenheitsform kann – muss aber meist nicht – in das Past Perfect verschoben werden.

"I **phoned** you." ➡ Ron said he **phoned / had phoned** me.

would, could, might und should bleiben unverändert.

"It **would / could / might** rain." ➡ They said it **would / could / might** rain.

Indirekte Rede (2)

Zeitverschiebung Teil 2

1. Kreuzen Sie die richtige Form an.

a "I'm just reading your letter." ➡ When I phoned, she said that she ... my letter.
- ☐ is just reading
- ☐ was just reading

b "I can't drive you to the airport."
➡ Pete said he ... , so Alan took me.
- ☐ can't drive me to the airport.
- ☐ couldn't drive me to the airport.

c "I wouldn't invite Terry."
➡ My friend said she ... Terry.
- ☐ won't invite
- ☐ wouldn't invite

d "I've sent a fax."
➡ Yesterday he said he ... a fax.
- ☐ has sent
- ☐ had sent

e "I'll bring a bottle of wine."
➡ Ben said he ... a bottle of wine.
- ☐ brings
- ☐ would bring

f "I might go to a movie." ➡ My daughter said she ... to a movie.
- ☐ might go
- ☐ mighted go

2. Setzen Sie in die indirekte Rede mit Zeitverschiebung.

a "I can't find my keys." ➡ Ann said ______

b "Tina is learning Chinese." ➡ My friend said that ______

c "We will need some extra chairs." ➡ Our neighbours said that ______

______

d "It isn't raining." ➡ Wally said ______

e "I'll phone the travel agent." ➡ Fred said ______

f "Tom's lost his passport." ➡ Pippa said her husband ______

g "We've bought a caravan." ➡ Sonia said that ______

3. Vorbereitungen für ein Fest. Berichten Sie, wer was zugesagt hatte.

Dave: "I'll warn the neighbours." *Dave said he would warn the neighbours.*

a Margie: "I've written the invitations." ______

b Mark: "I'll buy the wine." ______

c Sheila: "I can borrow some chairs." ______

d Philip: "I'll make a curry." ______

e Mary: "I've booked the band." ______

f Anita: "I'm trying to book a clown." ______

4. Übersetzen Sie. (Überlegen Sie zunächst, was wörtlich gesagt wurde.)

a Der Mann sagte, er riefe später zurück.

b Der Kunde sagte, er könne nicht bezahlen, weil er nicht genug Geld habe.

c Gregor sagte, er habe sein Bestes getan.

d Die Frau sagte, sie warte [gerade][1] auf einen Anruf.

e Seine Sekretärin sagte, er spreche [gerade][1] auf dem anderen Apparat *(phone)*.

f Tom sagte, ich könne sein Auto nehmen.

[1] Wörter in eckigen Klammern müssen nicht übersetzt werden.

54

I thought he would forget.

Ich dachte, er würde es vergessen.

I thought he would …

Auch Gedanken können wir mit der indirekten Rede wiedergeben. Und nicht nur Gedanken – auch Beschwerden, Versprechungen usw. Dazu verwenden wir besondere Verben, wie z. B. think, complain, promise etc. (Es wäre ja auch eintönig, wenn wir immer nur said, said, said sagten.)

In dieser Unit beschäftigen wir uns also mit weiteren Berichtsverben, allen voran mit tell.

Regel Anstelle von said können wir meist told zur Einleitung der indirekten Rede verwenden. Es gibt aber einen wichtigen Unterschied:

– said verwenden wir in der Regel ohne die Person zu nennen, der etwas gesagt wurde.[1]

– told können wir nur mit Nennung der Person verwenden.

David **said** that (~~said me that~~) he knew Tom Cruise.

David **told** me that (~~told that~~) he knew Tom Cruise.

Auch mit vielen anderen Verben können wir die indirekte Rede einleiten.

John denkt: "**I've** spent too much." ➡ John **thought** (that) he **had** spent too much.
John dachte, er habe zu viel ausgegeben.

Peter hofft: "Perhaps **I'll** see Ann." ➡ Peter **hoped** (that) he **would** see Ann.
Peter hoffte, dass er Ann sehen würde.

Tina beschwert sich: "You'**re** late." ➡ Tina **complained** (that) I **was** late.
Tina beschwerte sich, dass ich zu spät käme.

Ann verspricht: "I'**ll** book a table." ➡ Ann **promised** (that) she **would** book a table.
Ann versprach, dass sie einen Tisch bestellen würde.

---

[1]Möglich, aber seltener ist said + to + Person (David said to me that …).

Indirekte Rede (3)

said, told und andere Berichtsverben

1. Kreuzen Sie die richtige Form an.

a Tony ... he was at a fantastic party last weekend.
- ☐ told
- ☐ told me

b The Smiths ... that they knew a lovely little restaurant on the coast.
- ☐ said
- ☐ said us

c Who ... that I was leaving the firm?
- ☐ said you
- ☐ told you

d Robert complained that we ... squash for over a year.
- ☐ don't play
- ☐ hadn't played

e Tom promised that he ... , but he didn't.
- ☐ will phone
- ☐ would phone

f I hoped that I ... more, but I didn't.
- ☐ find out
- ☐ would find out

2. Ergänzen Sie say / said oder tell / told.

a That's not true! Who ________________ that?
b What did the boss ________________? Did he agree?
c We waited before we ________________ our children about our holiday plans.
d I didn't ________________ that you were a stupid old fool. That is a misunderstanding.
e How are we going to ________________ him that his wife is dead?
f Did you ________________ anybody what you saw?

3. Setzen Sie in die indirekte Rede.

a "This food is cold." ➡ The customer complained ________________________________

____

b "Have they arrived safely?" ➡ Ann hoped ________________________________
c "A hotel room in London will be very expensive." ➡ Glenn thought ________________

____

d "I'll pay you back when we get home." ➡ John promised ________________________

____

e "I've found the perfect job." ➡ Sally thought ________________________________
f "It's raining again." ➡ The children complained ________________________________

4. Übersetzen Sie.

a Er sagte seiner Lehrerin, dass er seine Hausaufgaben vergessen habe.
b Ich sagte, dass ich nicht hungrig sei.
c Sie haben mir versprochen, dass Sie am Freitag liefern *(deliver)* würden.
d Ich sagte, dass ich keine Zeit hätte.
e Ich dachte, ich hätte das Fenster geschlossen.
f Wir haben ihm gesagt, dass er für die Stelle zu alt sei.

55 I only asked him if he liked my mouse.

Ich habe ihn doch nur gefragt, ob er meine Maus mögen würde.

I asked if he liked ...

Tinas Neffe wird wörtlich gefragt haben:
"Do you like my mouse?"
(„Magst du meine Maus?").
In der indirekten Rede wird diese Frage mit asked if eingeleitet, die Umschreibung mit do verschwindet und die Zeitform des Verbs wird „verschoben".
In dieser Unit geht es um Fragen in der indirekten Rede.

Regel Fragen geben wir in der indirekten Rede mit ask if / whether (= „ob") oder mit ask + Fragewort wieder. (Nach ask steht kein Komma!) Die Zeiten werden „verschoben" (→ Unit 53).

"Is Peter ill?" ➡ Laura asked if / whether Peter **was** ill.
Laura fragte, ob Peter krank sei.

"**Can** I help?" ➡ Ben asked if / whether he **could** help.
Ben fragte, ob er helfen könne.

"**Have** you met Frank?" ➡ David asked if / whether I **had** met Frank.
David fragte, ob ich Frank kennen gelernt hätte.

"**Will** it snow?" ➡ The children asked if / whether it **would** snow.
Die Kinder fragten, ob es schneien würde.

"How **are** you feeling?" ➡ Ann asked how I **was** feeling.
Ann fragte, wie ich mich fühlte.

Eine Umschreibung mit do / does / did verwenden wir in indirekten Fragen nicht.

"Do you **know** Eileen?" ➡ Tom asked me if / whether I **knew** Eileen.
"What **does** it **cost**?" ➡ The customer asked what it **cost**.
"Did you **win**?" ➡ My friends all asked me if / whether I **had won**.

! Beachten Sie die Satzstellung.

"When is your birthday?" ➡ Tina asked me when my birthday was.
(... asked me ~~when was my birthday~~.)

"How expensive was the hotel?" ➡ They asked me how expensive the hotel was.
(... asked me ~~how expensive was the hotel~~.)

Die Wiedergabe von Bitten, Aufforderungen und Befehlen in der indirekten Rede erfolgt mit ask / tell sb to do sth (→ Units 50–51).

1. Kreuzen Sie die richtige Form an.

a The boy asked me if I … mice.
☐ did like
☐ liked

b Some tourists asked me if I … show them the way.
☐ can
☐ could

c My boss asked me where … .
☐ my report was
☐ was my report

d Tina asked us … .
☐ when the film did start
☐ when the film started

e I … smoked.
☐ asked Tom, if he
☐ asked Tom if he

f We asked who … the internet address.
☐ did know
☐ knew

2. Geben Sie die Fragen in der indirekten Rede wieder.

a Is the road icy?
b Has anyone called the police?
c Is the road blocked?
d Have you given First Aid?

e What has happened?
f Who saw the accident?
g Who is going to pay for the repair?
h How many people are hurt?

a My colleague in the back of the car asked me *if / whether the road was icy.*
b A man asked me ______
c The police asked ______
d Someone asked me ______
e My wife asked me *what* ______
f The police asked ______
g The other driver asked ______
h A reporter from the newspaper asked ______

3. Berichten Sie von Ihrem Vorstellungsgespräch.

a "How old are you?" ➡ They asked me ______
b "Do you speak English?" ➡ They asked me ______
c "How long have you been in your present job?" ➡ They asked me ______
______
d "What do you hope to earn?" ➡ They asked me ______
e "Will you be prepared to work at weekends?" ➡ They asked me ______
______
f "How did you hear about the job?" ➡ They asked me ______

56 If you remember.

Wenn du daran denkst.

when … if …

Tim sagt, er werde die Wäsche aufhängen, wenn die Sendung vorbei ist. Tina denkt sich: „Wenn du daran denkst." Im Deutschen heißt es zweimal „wenn", im Englischen einmal when, einmal if. Mit dieser Unit beginnen wir das Thema der if-Sätze (Fortsetzung: Units 57–58) und schauen uns zunächst den Unterschied zwischen if und when an.

Regel

if entspricht „wenn" im Sinne von „falls".
when entspricht „wenn" im zeitlichen Sinne („dann, wann").

if = falls	**If** you want, I can drive you home. *Wenn du willst, kann ich dich heimfahren.*
when = dann, wann	**When** the exam is finished, I'll feel better. *Wenn die Prüfung vorbei ist, werde ich mich besser fühlen.*

In der Bedeutung „jedes Mal, wenn", „immer, wenn" können wir wahlweise if oder when verwenden.

If / When we win a match, I feel good. *Wenn wir ein Spiel gewinnen, fühle ich mich gut.*

if und when können am Satzanfang oder in der Satzmitte stehen. Stehen sie am Satzanfang, setzen wir meist ein Komma.

if / when am Satzanfang: Komma	if / when in der Satzmitte: kein Komma
If Peter phones, please tell me.	Please tell me if Peter phones.
When Ann comes, we'll start.	We'll start when Ann comes.

! Beachten Sie die Verbformen in diesen Sätzen mit when:

when = „dann, wann"	When Ann **comes**, we'**ll start** (~~we start~~) this meeting. *[einfache Gegenwart – will-Zukunft]*
when = „immer wenn"	When we **win**, I **feel** happy. *[einfache Gegenwart in beiden Satzhälften]*

Auf die Verbformen in if-Sätzen gehen wir in den Units 57–58 genau ein.

1. Kreuzen Sie die richtige Form an.

a We can discuss it later ... you don't have time now.
- ☐ if
- ☐ when

b ... the concert finishes, we can go for a drink at Enzo's.
- ☐ If
- ☐ When

c ... we're late, don't wait. Start without us.
- ☐ If
- ☐ When

d You can use my mobile ... if your battery is empty.
- ☐ phone,
- ☐ phone

e When I ... Tony at the meeting, I'll ask him about his tent.
- ☐ see
- ☐ will see

f When I see a big dog, I ... frightened.
- ☐ feel
- ☐ will feel

2. Ergänzen Sie if oder when.

a Is it OK ________________ I bring a friend to your party?
b ________________ the weather stays good, we can go surfing this weekend.
c Angela should be here soon. We'll eat ________________ she gets here.
d ________________ the film is good, we can take your parents to it next week.
e ________________ the train is late, I always miss my bus.
f ________________ the train is late, just take a taxi.

3. Bilden Sie Sätze mit if und when.

It might rain. ➡ *If it rains,* we'll have the party indoors.
I don't know the price yet. ➡ *When I know the price,* I'll order some tickets.

a The eggs aren't ready. ➡ ______________________________, we'll have breakfast.
b We might need more money. ➡ ______________________________, we can always ask Bill to lend us some.
c That policeman might speak English. ➡ ______________________________, we can ask him the way.
d I don't feel strong enough. ➡ ______________________________, I'll go back to work.
e You might have time. ➡ ______________________________, you should visit the old castle.
f Mr Smith hasn't arrived. ➡ ______________________________, I'll ask him to call you back.

4. Übersetzen Sie.

a Wenn du heute Abend gehst, lass bitte das Licht an.
b Wenn ich nicht da bin, versuch es später noch einmal.
c Bring Tony [mit][1], wenn er Zeit hat.
d Wenn wir unsere neue Wohnung haben, geben wir eine große Party.
e Wenn der Wein mehr als 10 Euro kostet, kauf ihn nicht.
f Wenn wir nach Hause kommen, mache ich etwas zu essen.

[1] Wörter in eckigen Klammern müssen nicht übersetzt werden.

57 If he tells that story again, I'll scream.

Wenn er diese Geschichte noch einmal erzählt, schreie ich.

If he tells . . ., I'll . . .

Es sieht sehr danach aus, dass Tims Vater einen uralten Witz wieder zum Besten geben will. Dass er dies tun wird, ist vorstellbar, wahrscheinlich, fast schon Tatsache. Tina sagt, was dann als Folge geschehen wird.

Sie verwendet einen Satz mit if, einen so genannten Bedingungssatz. In einem Bedingungssatz sagen wir, was unter bestimmten Umständen geschehen wird. Ein Bedingungssatz besteht aus einem if-Teil (die Bedingung) und einem Ergebnis-Teil (die Folge):

Bedingung	Wenn er diesen Witz noch einmal erzählt,
Folge	dann schreie ich.

Regel Wenn wir von Bedingungen sprechen, die vorstellbar, wahrscheinlich oder fast schon Tatsache sind, verwenden wir im if-Teil die einfache Gegenwart, für die Folge will / won't.

Bedingung	Folge
If you **wait**,	I'll show you the way. *Wenn du wartest, zeige ich dir den Weg.*
If it **snows**,	we **won't** go. *Wenn es schneit, fahren wir nicht.*
If you **don't mind**,	I'll answer that question later. *Wenn Sie nichts dagegen haben, beantworte ich diese Frage später.*
If they **don't agree**,	what **will** you do? *Wenn sie nicht einverstanden sind, was wirst du tun?*

Im Folge-Teil kann auch can / must / might oder die Befehlsform stehen.

If he **phones**,	you **can / must / might** find out the address. *Wenn er anruft, kannst / musst / könntest du die Adresse herausfinden.*
If he **phones**,	**ask** him for the address. *Wenn er anruft, frag ihn nach der Adresse.*

! Im if-Teil kann will nicht stehen – nur in der Folge!

If the boss **finds out** (~~will find out~~), he **will be** very angry.
Wenn der Chef es herausfindet, wird er sehr böse sein.

1. Kreuzen Sie die richtige Form an.

a If it … before Saturday, that will be early enough.
- ☐ arrives
- ☐ will arrive

b They won't understand you if you … Bavarian.
- ☐ speak
- ☐ will speak

c If we … now, we won't be there in time.
- ☐ don't leave
- ☐ won't leave

d If she … that again, I'll explode!
- ☐ says
- ☐ will say

e I'll take a taxi if the train … late.
- ☐ is
- ☐ will be

f What … they say if we don't go to the meeting?
- ☐ do
- ☐ will

2. Korrigieren Sie.

a If it ~~will be~~ too expensive, we won't go. ______

b I ~~ask~~ Donna if I see her. ______

c It won't be easy if our best player ~~will be~~ ill. ______

d He ~~doesn't get~~ the job if he doesn't dress better for the interview. ______

e What ~~do you do~~ if they say 'no'? ______

f She ~~tells~~ Adrian if she finds out more. ______

3. Bilden Sie Sätze wie im Beispiel.

If the weather / be / bad tomorrow, we / do / something else.
If the weather is bad tomorrow, we'll do something else.

a If you / drink / this, you / feel / better. ______

b If I / not like / it, I / order / something else. ______

c We / keep / it here for you if you / not want / to take it with you now. ______

d If you / not tell / him soon, he / find out / from someone else. ______

e It / not be / a problem if you / ask nicely. ______

f If the phone / ring, / I / answer / it. ______

4. Übersetzen Sie.

a Wenn du jetzt ins Bett gehst, wirst du [dich][1] morgen besser fühlen.

b Wenn ich genug Geld habe, werde ich Champagner kaufen.

c Ich mache die Sandwiches, wenn du willst.

d Wenn du willst, kannst du hier schlafen.

e Wenn es noch einmal passiert, wirst du die Polizei rufen?

f Wenn wir nicht schneller arbeiten, sind wir um 12.00 Uhr [noch][1] nicht fertig *(finished)*.

[1]Wörter in eckigen Klammern müssen nicht übersetzt werden.

If his jokes were funny, I wouldn't mind.

Wenn seine Witze komisch wären, würde es mir nichts ausmachen.

If … were … , … would …

In ihrem Bedingungssatz mit if spekuliert Tina und sagt, was wäre, wenn die Dinge anders lägen:

BEDINGUNG Wenn seine Witze komisch wären,

FOLGE dann würde es mir nichts ausmachen.

Tatsächlich sind die Witze aber nicht gut, sondern schrecklich.

In dieser Unit geht es um Tatbestände, die nicht der Wirklichkeit entsprechen, und wie man in einem Bedingungssatz darüber redet.

Regel Wenn wir von Bedingungen sprechen, die unwahrscheinlich oder unmöglich oder reine Spekulation sind, verwenden wir im if-Teil die einfache Vergangenheit (für etwas Gegenwärtiges oder Zukünftiges), für die Folge would. (Die Kurzform von would ist 'd.)

Bedingung	Folge
If I **won** $1 million,	I **would** stop working.

Wenn ich 1 Million $ gewinnen würde, würde ich aufhören zu arbeiten.
[Aber es ist unwahrscheinlich, dass ich jemals eine Million gewinnen werde.]

If it **didn't cost** so much,	**I'd** probably buy it.

Wenn es nicht so viel kosten würde, würde ich es wahrscheinlich kaufen.
[Aber es kostet zu viel, ist zu teuer.]

If you **were** a woman,	**would** you think this is fair?

Wenn du eine Frau wärest, würdest du das für fair halten?
[Aber du bist keine Frau, sondern ein Mann.]

In der Folge kann auch could oder might stehen.

If you **spoke** French,	you **could** translate this letter for me.

Wenn du Französisch sprechen würdest, könntest du mir diesen Brief übersetzen.
[Aber du kannst ja kein Französisch.]

! Im *if*-Teil kann would nicht stehen – nur in der Folge!

If you **loved** (~~would love~~) me, you **wouldn't say** that.

Wenn du mich lieben würdest, würdest du das nicht sagen.

1. Kreuzen Sie die richtige Form an.

a If I ... a dog, I would sleep all day.
- am
- was

b If you ... a ghost, what would you do?
- saw
- would see

c If I was 10 years younger, I ... and get another job.
- leave
- would leave

d If I ... a Rolls Royce, I would be afraid that someone might steal it.
- owned
- would own

e What would you do if the other firm ... you more money?
- offered
- would offer

f If Tina ... her aerobics every day, she wouldn't be so fit.
- didn't do
- wouldn't do

2. Ergänzen Sie.

a If I gave up smoking, I ________________ *(save)* a lot of money.
b If I ________________ *(save)* a lot of money, I could go on exotic holidays.
c If I ________________ *(go)* on exotic holidays, I might fly to places like Cuba.
d If I ________________ *(fly)* to Cuba, I might buy some Cuban cigars.
e If I ________________ *(buy)* some Cuban cigars, I ________________ *(try)* one.
f If the cigar ________________ *(be)* good, I ________________ *(start)* smoking again, I expect.

3. Bilden Sie Sätze wie im Beispiel.

If you / drink / less alcohol, you / be / healthier.
If you drank less alcohol, you would be healthier.

a If you / work / harder, you / earn / more money.
____

b If he / go / to bed earlier, he / not be / so tired in the morning.
____

c If you / know / the name of the street, it / help.
____

d If you / find / a job in Australia or the USA, / you go?
____

4. Übersetzen Sie

a Wenn ich mehr Geld hätte, würde ich eine größere Wohnung nehmen.
b Wenn ich jünger wäre, würde ich Bungeejumping probieren *(try)*.
c Wenn ich die Antwort wüsste, würde ich [sie][1] dir sagen.
d Wenn du Ann fragen würdest, könnte sie dir helfen.
e Es wäre besser, wenn du den Chef heute nicht fragen würdest.

[1]Wörter in eckigen Klammern müssen nicht übersetzt werden.

59 The orchestra is playing beautifully.

Das Orchester spielt schön.

beautiful – beautifully

Tim soll aufwachen, der Tanz sei so schön. Er aber gibt an, die Augen geschlossen zu haben, um der Musik zu lauschen: Das Orchester spiele so schön.

Unser Cartoontext zeigt einen wesentlichen Unterschied zwischen deutschem und englischem Sprachgebrauch: zweimal heißt es im Deutschen „schön", im Englischen dagegen einmal beautiful, das andere Mal beautifully.

Es geht um den Unterschied zwischen Adjektiv und Adverb. Vorweg wollen wir diese Begriffe einmal klären.

Mit einem Adjektiv beschreiben wir eine Person oder Sache und sagen, wie die Person/Sache ist. Ein Adjektiv verwenden wir vor einem Nomen (1) oder nach einer Form des Verbs be (2):

I saw a **beautiful** sunset last week. (1) The sunset **was beautiful**. (2)

Ich sah letzte Woche einen schönen Sonnenuntergang. Der Sonnenuntergang war schön.

Mit einem Adverb sagen wir, wie etwas gemacht wird. Wir bestimmen ein Verb näher:

They are dancing **beautifully**. The orchestra is playing **beautifully**.

Sie tanzen schön. Das Orchester spielt schön.

Regel Adjektiv und Adverb haben im Englischen (bis auf wenige Ausnahmen → Unit 60) eine unterschiedliche Form. Adverbien leitet man vom Adjektiv ab, indem man die Endung -ly anhängt.

Tina is **careful**. She works **carefully**. *Tina ist sorgfältig. Sie arbeitet sorgfältig.*

Tina is **nice**. She asked me so **nicely**. *Tina ist nett. Sie bat mich so nett.*

Achten Sie auf diese Besonderheiten:

- Konsonant + y + ly ➡ Konsonant + ily: easy ➡ easily
- Endung le + ly ➡ ly: possible ➡ possibly
- Endung ic + ly ➡ ically: automatic ➡ automatic**ally**

1. Kreuzen Sie die richtige Form an.

a My boss is a … person.
- ☐ nice
- ☐ nicely

b She isn't speaking very … .
- ☐ clear
- ☐ clearly

c His father spoke to him … .
- ☐ angry
- ☐ angrily

d Henry is a … driver.
- ☐ dangerous
- ☐ dangerously

e Why does he always work so …?
- ☐ slow
- ☐ slowly

f Sorry, that date is … for me.
- ☐ impossible
- ☐ impossibly

2. Ergänzen Sie ein Adverb mit -ly.

I'm a slow worker. I work _slowly_.

a We have regular meetings. We meet ______________ every month.
b It's an easy test. You will be able to answer the questions ______________.
c You're a careful driver. You always drive so ______________.
d He's a very polite person. He always behaves so ______________.
e It's an automatic kettle. It stops ______________ when the water boils.
f The rain was heavy. It rained ______________ all day.

3. Adjektiv oder Adverb? Ergänzen Sie die richtige Form.

You must remember. We met at a (a) ______________ *(big)* party at Rob and Ann's house. I was standing (b) ______________ *(quiet)* at the bar, and I was (c) ______________ *(slow)* getting drunk, when you came for a (d) ______________ *(quick)* drink. You were dancing (e) ______________ *(wild)* most of the time, so you were very (f) ______________ *(thirsty)*. Someone next to you (g) ______________ *(stupid)* knocked their glass over. You (h) ______________ *(automatic)* took a step backwards and stepped on my foot. It all happened so (i) ______________ *(sudden)*. I was already quite (j) ______________ *(drunk)* and I (k) ______________ *(simple)* threw my drink at you. You (l) ______________ *(probable)* wanted to hit me, but you behaved so (m) ______________ *(polite)*. You said, "Oh, your glass is empty. Let me get you another drink."

4. Übersetzen Sie. Sie brauchen die folgenden Adjektive und die entsprechenden Adverbien: bad, happy, perfect.

a Helga ist die perfekte Sekretärin.
b Ich habe schlecht geschlafen.
c Bist du glücklich in deinem neuen Job?
d Es war ein schlechtes Hotel.
e Die Kinder haben sich perfekt benommen *(behave)*.
f Der Gewinner lächelte glücklich.

He paints very well.

Er malt sehr gut.

good – well

Unser Cartoontext verdeutlicht eine häufige Fehlerquelle für uns Deutschsprachige: Das zu good gehörige Adverb heißt well:

Dieses Bild ist gut. = This picture is good.

Er malt gut. = He paints well (nicht: He paints ~~good~~).

Regel Nicht alle Adverbien werden durch Anhängen von -ly gebildet. Einige haben besondere Formen.

1. Zu dem Adjektiv good gehört das Adverb well.

Tim is a **good** cook. He cooks **well**. *Tim ist ein guter Koch. Er kocht gut.*

2. Ein paar Adverbien haben die gleiche Form wie das Adjektiv.

The **early** train is never full, so I travel **early**. *Der Frühzug ist nie voll, also fahre ich früh.*
Tim is a **fast** driver. He drives **fast**. *Tim ist ein schneller Fahrer. Er fährt schnell.*
It was a **late** flight. I arrived **late**. *Es war ein später Flug. Ich kam spät an.*
Ron is a **hard** worker. He works **hard**. *Ron ist ein fleißiger Mitarbeiter. Er arbeitet fleißig.*

! Nicht verwechseln: late (spät) – lately (in letzter Zeit), hard (hart, schwer) – hardly (kaum).

Henry got up **late**. He has done that often **lately**.
Henry stand spät auf. Das hat er in letzter Zeit oft getan.
I worked **hard** today. I **hardly** had time for a coffee break.
Ich habe heute hart gearbeitet. Ich hatte kaum Zeit für eine Kaffeepause.

Ein Adverb kann sich auch auf ein Adjektiv oder ein anderes Adverb beziehen.

The new model is **extremely** expensive. *Das neue Modell ist extrem teuer.*
It's **unusually** warm today. *Es ist heute ungewöhnlich warm.*

Peter works **awfully** slowly. *Peter arbeitet furchtbar langsam.*
The tickets are selling **extremely** fast. *Die Karten verkaufen sich äußerst schnell.*

1. Kreuzen Sie die richtige Form an.

a You speak English … .
- ☐ good
- ☐ well

b Your English is very … .
- ☐ good
- ☐ well

c Ann trains very … .
- ☐ hard
- ☐ hardly

d It's … unusual to see a wolf in Europe.
- ☐ extreme
- ☐ extremely

e We arrived … . It was almost midnight.
- ☐ late
- ☐ lately

f Why should I lend you 20 euros? I … know you.
- ☐ hard
- ☐ hardly

2. Ergänzen Sie good oder well.

a I thought you were ________________. You played very ________________.
b It's a ________________ book. The author writes extremely ________________.
c You answered that question ________________. That was very ________________. Two extra points.
d I'm not explaining this very ________________. It wasn't a very ________________ explanation.
e Do they pay ________________? – No, the money is not ________________.
f The interview went ________________. I was ________________ prepared.

3. Ergänzen Sie die richtige Form.

a I haven't had much free time ________________ *(late / lately).*
b I've been working very ________________ *(hard / hardly)* at the office.
c Life has been ________________ *(extreme / extremely)* stressful.
d I've ________________ *(hard / hardly)* had a moment to myself.
e I am ________________ *(awful / awfully)* tired.
f I am also becoming ________________ *(terrible / terribly)* boring. I can only talk about work!

4. Übersetzen Sie.

a Du singst sehr gut und sehr schön.
b Mein Chef fährt schnell. Er fährt gefährlich.
c Ich kenne London gut.
d Tony geht spät ins Bett und steht früh auf.
e Das Wetter war ungewöhnlich warm.
f Emma spielt [gerade][1] sehr gut.

[1]Wörter in eckigen Klammern müssen nicht übersetzt werden.

61

He's younger than she is.

Er ist jünger als sie.

younger than

In dieser Unit geht es um Vergleiche („Er ist viel jünger als sie"). Der Cartoontext illustriert gleich einen wichtigen Unterschied: Im Deutschen heißt es „jünger als", im Englischen aber younger than (nicht ~~younger as~~)!

Regel Vergleiche drücken wir mit than aus.

Dave is 28, Janet is 30. Dave is **younger than** Janet. *Dave ist jünger als Janet.*
The train is **cheaper than** the plane. *Der Zug ist billiger als das Flugzeug.*

Wir bilden die Vergleichsform von Adjektiven (den so genannten Komparativ) auf diese Weise:

1. Kurze Adjektive (eine Silbe): -er anhängen:
   cheap – **cheaper** *billig – billiger*
   slow – **slower** *langsam – langsamer*
   nice – **nicer** *nett – netter*
   late – **later** *spät – später*
   Beachten Sie: Verdopplung des Endkonsonanten bei z. B.:
   big – **bigger** *groß – größer*
   fat – **fatter** *dick – dicker*
   hot – **hotter** *heiß – heißer*
   thin – **thinner** *dünn – dünner*
2. Zweisilbige Adjektive auf -y: -er anhängen, y wird zu i:
   easy – **easier** *leicht – leichter*
   funny – **funnier** *lustig – lustiger*
   Ebenso: angry (zornig), crazy (verrückt), early (früh), happy (glücklich), heavy (schwer)
3. Andere zwei- sowie drei- und mehrsilbige Adjektive: more voranstellen:
   interesting – **more interesting** *interessant – interessanter*
   exciting – **more exciting** *aufregend – aufregender*
   Shows are **more interesting** than sport. *Shows sind interessanter als Sport.*
   The film is **more exciting** than the book. *Der Film ist aufregender als das Buch.*
4. good – **better** *gut – besser*
   bad – **worse** *schlimm – schlimmer*
   Today's test was **worse**, not **better**. *Der heutige Test war schlimmer, nicht besser.*

1. Kreuzen Sie die richtige Form an.

a People in the west are .... .
- ☐ more rich
- ☐ richer

b London is ... than Berlin.
- ☐ biger
- ☐ bigger

c This hotel is ... than the Hilton.
- ☐ exclusiver
- ☐ more exclusive

d The brown pair is cheaper ... the black pair.
- ☐ as
- ☐ than

e The weather is ... than yesterday.
- ☐ badder
- ☐ worse

f I'm ... than I was last year.
- ☐ happier
- ☐ happyer

2. Ergänzen Sie die Vergleichsform.

a	old	*older*	f	important	______	k	difficult	______
b	expensive	*more expensive*	g	famous	______	l	heavy	______
c	hard	______	h	bad	______	m	thin	______
d	quick	______	i	crazy	______	n	careful	______
e	interesting	______	j	easy	______	o	good	______

3. Vergleichen Sie. Bilden Sie jeweils zwei Sätze.

Ann is 10. Joey is 8. *(old / young)* *Ann is older than Joey. / Joey is younger than Ann.*

a It's 1 hour by air, 4 hours by train. *(fast / slow)*
The plane is ______
The train is ______

b Steak costs 15 euros, salmon costs 12 euros. *(expensive / cheap)*
Steak is ______
Salmon is ______

c Football is awful. Tennis is OK. *(boring / interesting)*
Football is ______
Tennis is ______

d I hate Monday. I like Friday. *(bad / good)*
Monday is ______
Friday is ______

4. Übersetzen Sie. Sie brauchen folgende Adjektive: bad, easy, exciting, expensive, surprised, tall.

a Ich bin größer als du.
b Dieses Restaurant ist viel teurer als McDonald's.
c Der Verkehr gestern war schlimmer als heute.
d Dieses Problem ist leichter zu lösen *(solve)*.
e Ein Livekonzert ist aufregender als eine CD.
f Wer war überraschter – du oder dein Chef?

62 The oldest profession in the world.

Das älteste Gewerbe der Welt.

the oldest …

Jede(r) weiß, was mit the oldest profession (das älteste Gewerbe) gemeint ist. Uns interessiert dabei die Form the oldest, mit der Endung -est. In dieser Unit geht es um die höchste Steigerungsstufe bei Adjektiven, den so genannten Superlativ. Und jede(r) weiß, was gemeint ist, wenn in der Werbung von Superlativen gesprochen wird: das größte, das beste, das schönste …

Regel Die Superlativform von Adjektiven bilden wir auf folgende Weise:

1. Adjektive, die den Komparativ (→ Unit 61) mit -er bilden: -est anhängen:
   old, older, **(the) oldest** young, younger, **(the) youngest**
   easy, easier, **(the) easiest** funny, funnier, **(the) funniest**
   Beachten Sie: Verdopplung des Endkonsonanten bei z. B.:
   big, bigger, **(the) biggest** hot, hotter, **(the) hottest**

2. Adjektive, die den Komparativ mit more bilden: most voranstellen:
   interesting, more interesting, **(the) most interesting**
   exciting, more exciting, **(the) most exciting**

3. good, better, **(the) best** bad, worse, **(the) worst**

Wenn in einem Vergleich zwei Personen oder Dinge gleichwertig sind, verwenden wir die Grundform des Adjektivs mit as … as. Verwechseln Sie nicht as und than!

Sarah is 26. Tony is 28, Ariana is 28.
Tony is older **than** (~~as~~) Sarah. *Tony ist älter als Sarah.*
Tony is **as** old **as** Ariana. *Tony ist so alt wie Ariana.*
But Sarah isn't **as** old **as** Ariana. *Aber Sarah ist nicht so alt wie Ariana.*

Auch nach the same („der/die/das gleiche“, „der-/die-/dasselbe“) verwenden wir as.
I like **the same** things as Sarah. *Ich mag die gleichen Sachen wie Sarah.*

1. Ergänzen Sie die Superlativform.

Which is ______________ *(large)* city in the world?
Which is *the largest* city in the world?

a This is ______________ *(boring)* film I've ever seen.
b It was ______________ *(good)* hotel we've ever stayed in.
c Death Valley is ______________ *(hot)* place I've ever been to.
d It was ______________ *(bad)* accident the police have seen.
e I think I am ______________ *(lucky)* person alive.
f What is ______________ *(interesting)* job you've ever had?

2. Bilden Sie Sätze mit ... is as ... as ... oder mit ... isn't as ... as ... .

Sonia is 21, Tom is 21. *(old)* *Sonia is as old as Tom.*
Sonia is 21. Dave is 23. *(old)* *Sonia isn't as old as Dave.*

a It's 25 °C today. It was 25 °C yesterday. *(warm)*
The weather today ______________ yesterday.
b It's cloudy today. It rained yesterday. *(bad)*
The weather today ______________ yesterday.
c Jack is 1 metre 73. Tony is 1 metre 78. *(tall)*
Jack ______________ Tony.
d The Excelsior is exclusive. The Bristol Hotel is exclusive, too. *(exclusive)*
The Excelsior ______________ the Bristol.
e Steel is hard. A diamond is harder. *(hard)*
Steel ______________ a diamond.
f From city centre to city centre it's 2 hours by train, and 2 hours by plane, too. *(fast)*
Going by train ______________ going by plane.

3. as oder than? Ergänzen Sie.

a Their car is bigger ______________ our car.
b My English is quite good. My French isn't ______________ good.
c The situation is worse ______________ last year.
d I know your office is bigger, but it isn't ______________ nice.
e Baxter is a good player, but she isn't as fast ______________ Walters.
f I am more hopeful ______________ I was that we will win.

4. Übersetzen Sie.

a Gestern war der heißeste Tag des Jahres.
b Die Jahre in London waren die glücklichsten meines Lebens.
c Er trägt die gleichen Schuhe wie du.
d Der Preis ist nicht so wichtig wie die Qualität.
e Montag ist der schlimmste Tag der Woche.

63 We haven't seen any bears.

Wir haben keine Bären gesehen.

some ... any

I can see <u>some</u> elks („einige Elche"); we have<u>n't</u> seen <u>any</u> bears at all („wir haben überhaupt keine Bären gesehen"). In dieser Unit geht es um die Mengenbezeichnungen some und any.

Regel some verwenden wir in bejahten, d. h. positiven Sätzen; not ... any in verneinten Sätzen. some bedeutet „etwas / einige", wird aber im Deutschen oft nicht übersetzt. not ... any entspricht „kein(e)".

We have **some** whisky. We don't have **any** gin. *Wir haben (etwas) Whisky. Wir haben keinen Gin.*

I have **some** euros. I don't have **any** dollars. *Ich habe (einige) Euro. Ich habe keine Dollar.*

They had **some** nice grapes. But I couldn't find **any** peaches. *Sie hatten (einige) schöne Trauben. Aber ich konnte keine Pfirsiche finden.*

In Fragen verwenden wir meist any. Wir gebrauchen jedoch some, wenn die Frage eine Bitte oder ein Angebot darstellt.

Is there **any** sugar? *Gibt es Zucker?*

Can you give me **any** details? *Können Sie mir irgendwelche Details nennen?*

Aber:

Bitte: Can I have **some** milk, please? *Kann ich bitte etwas Milch haben?*

Angebot: Shall I make **some** tea? *Soll ich (etwas) Tee kochen?*

1. Verneinen Sie diese Sätze.

They had some tulips. ➡ *They didn't have any tulips.*

a I've read some of her books. ➡ ______

b There are some interesting programmes on TV tonight. ➡ ______

______

c We have some contacts in Sweden. ➡ ______

d Tony made some notes. ➡ ______

e We need some batteries. ➡ ______

f I will see some old friends. ➡ ______

2. Bilden Sie zu den Sätzen in Übung 1 nun Fragen.

They had some tulips. ➡ *Did they have any tulips?*

a Have you read ______ of her books?

b Are there ______ on TV tonight?

c Do you ______?

d Did Tony ______?

e Do we ______?

f Will you ______?

3. Ergänzen Sie die Angebote.

This is heavy. – *(give you / help)* *Shall I give you some help?*

a I'm hungry. – *(make / sandwiches)* Shall I ______

b We need a break. – *(make / tea)* Shall I ______

c I'd like to know what the campsite looks like. – *(look for / photos)*
Shall I ______

d Everybody is sleepy. – *(open / windows)* ______

e Let's have a party. – *(phone / friends)* ______

f We need something as a present. – *(buy / flowers)* ______

4. Ergänzen Sie some oder any.

a Can we have ______ more bread, please?

b I need ______ more time.

c We're new. We don't know ______ people here.

d I don't watch ______ sport. I hate it.

e There aren't ______ really interesting places around here.

f Could we have ______ water, please?

g Will they need ______ other information?

In the morning, at breakfast time ...

Am Morgen, zur Frühstückszeit ...

in ... at ...

Ein romantisches Frühstück gibt es bei Tim und Tina nur im Radio. Uns interessieren an der Situation die kleinen Wörtchen („Präpositionen") at und in. Der unterschiedliche Gebrauch dieser Wörtchen im Deutschen und im Englischen ist immer wieder ein Stolperstein.

Regel In folgenden Zeitbestimmungen ist der Gebrauch der Präpositionen anders als im Deutschen.

Uhrzeit: at
at 6 o'clock *um 6 Uhr*
at half past three *um halb vier*
at midday *um Mittag*
at midnight *um Mitternacht*

Mahlzeiten: at
at breakfast *beim Frühstück*
at lunchtime *zur Mittagszeit*
at supper (time) *zum Abendessen*

Wochentage und Datum: on
on Monday (morning) *am Montag(morgen)*
on Saturday (evening) *am Samstag(abend)*
on 1st January *am 1. Januar*
on Wednesday 6th June *am Mittwoch, 6. Juni*

Tageszeit: in
in the morning / afternoon / evening *am Morgen / Nachmittag / Abend*
in the day(time) *am Tag*

Nachtzeit: at
at night *in der Nacht*
at sunset *bei Sonnenuntergang*

Wochenende: at (US auch: on)
at / on the weekend *am Wochenende*

Feste: at (= zum Fest) und on (= an einem ganz bestimmten Festtag)
at Christmas / Easter / New Year *zu Weihnachten / Ostern / Neujahr*
on Christmas Day / Easter Sunday / New Year's Day *am ersten Weihnachtstag / Ostersonntag / Neujahrstag*
on my birthday *an meinem Geburtstag*

„Zeitwörter": at
at the moment *im Augenblick / Moment*
at my age *in meinem Alter*
at the age of 18 *im Alter von 18 Jahren*
at the beginning / end *am Anfang / Ende*

! Bei this / that, next und last verwenden wir keine Präposition!
an diesem Montag = this Monday *am nächsten / letzten Dienstag* = next / last Tuesday

Jahreszahlen dagegen immer mit Präposition: He died **in** 1999. *Er starb (im Jahre) 1999.*

1. Kreuzen Sie die richtige Form an.

a I don't work ... the afternoon or ... the weekend.
- ☐ in ... at
- ☐ on ... on

b We arrived ... 5 o'clock ... the afternoon.
- ☐ at ... in
- ☐ on ... in

c What are you doing ... Saturday evening?
- ☐ in
- ☐ on

d I am working very hard ... the moment.
- ☐ at
- ☐ in

e Can we meet ... Friday?
- ☐ next
- ☐ on next

f Where will you be ... Christmas Day?
- ☐ at
- ☐ on

g My grandfather started work ... the age of 14.
- ☐ at
- ☐ in

h We went to Morocco ... year.
- ☐ in the last
- ☐ last

2. Ergänzen Sie at, in oder on.

a ______ 14th July
b ______ Friday
c ______ Thursday morning
d ______ two o'clock
e ______ the afternoon
f ______ 5.25
g ______ Christmas time
h ______ quarter past ten
i ______ 2001
j ______ tea time
k ______ the moment
l ______ your age
m ______ the evening
n ______ Sunday evening
o ______ night
p ______ 11th September 2001
q ______ the daytime
r ______ sunset

3. Ergänzen Sie at, in, on oder keine Präposition.

a The next meeting is ______ 17th March ______ 10.30 ______ the morning.
b ______ night of course there is less traffic than ______ the day.
c ______ the moment I haven't decided what I'm going to do ______ my birthday.
d My father retired ______ the age of 64 ______ 1998.
e The carnival season begins ______ 11th November, ______ 11.11 ______ the morning.
f I won't be here ______ next Monday.

4. Übersetzen Sie.

a Wir fliegen am Sonntagmorgen um halb sechs.
b Ich arbeite nachts.
c Am letzten Sonntag war ich in London.
d Ich habe keine Zeit im Moment.
e Tonys Vater ist gestorben – im Alter von 58.
f Was machst du an deinem Geburtstag?

65 I'm at Munich Airport.

Ich bin am Münchener Flughafen.

at … on … to

at Munich Airport (am Münchener Flughafen), on a plane (in einer Maschine), to Tunis (nach Tunis). In Unit 64 behandelten wir Präpositionen in Zeitbestimmungen; hier geht es um Präpositionen in Ortsbestimmungen.

Regel at und on verwenden wir wie folgt.

Einrichtungen, in denen man etwas Bestimmtes verrichtet: at
at the airport *am Flughafen*
at the station *am Bahnhof*
at the supermarket *im Supermarkt*
at the cinema *im Kino*
at the theatre *im Theater*
at the office *im Büro*
at the doctor's *beim Arzt*
at school *in der Schule*
at work *in der Arbeit*

„direkt neben" / „direkt vor": at
at the door *an der Tür*
at the window *am Fenster*
at the table *am Tisch*
at the computer *am Computer*
at the bus stop *an der Bushaltestelle*
at the traffic lights *an der Ampel*
at the exit *beim Ausgang*

Veranstaltungen: at
at a meeting *in einer Sitzung*
at a party *auf einer Party*
at a festival *auf / bei einem Festival*

Adresse, Zuhause: at
at home *zu Hause*
at 17 Tin Road *(in der) Tin Road, Nr. 17*
at Jane's (house) *bei Jane (zu Hause)*
at this address *an dieser Adresse*

auf einer Fläche (auch einer vertikalen!): on
on the wall *an der Wand*
on the door *an der Tür[oberfläche]*
on the beach *am Strand*
on the first floor *in der ersten Etage*

Kommunikationsmittel: on
on the phone *am Telefon*
on the radio / TV *im Radio / Fernsehen*
on the internet *im Internet*

! Beachten Sie die folgenden Ausdrücke:

go to school *in die / zur Schule gehen*
go to the cinema / theatre *ins Kino / Theater gehen*
go to a concert *in ein Konzert gehen*
go to bed *ins Bett gehen*

in the country *auf dem Land*
in a photo / picture *auf einem Foto / Bild*
in the world *auf der Welt*
in the sky *am Himmel*
a holiday by the sea *ein Urlaub am Meer*

1. Kreuzen Sie die richtige Form an.

a We went … a concert last weekend.
- [ ] in
- [ ] to

b What is that up there … the sky?
- [ ] at
- [ ] in
- [ ] on

c What can you see … the photo?
- [ ] at
- [ ] in
- [ ] on

d I wasn't … home last night; I was … Tina's.
- [ ] at … at
- [ ] at … by

e There was a lovely picture … the wall.
- [ ] at
- [ ] on

f My office is … the third floor.
- [ ] at
- [ ] in
- [ ] on

2. Ergänzen Sie at, by, in, on oder to.

a It's the highest mountain ________________ the world.
b She grew up in a small town ________________ the sea.
c David's ________________ the phone. He's talking to his boss.
d Have you always lived ________________ that address?
e I found the information ________________ the internet.
f Where did you go ________________ school?
g They live in a small village ________________ the country.
h Can you meet me ________________ the station?
i We were ________________ a great party last weekend.
j The other office is ________________ 52 Wendover Road.
k The accident happened while I was waiting ________________ the traffic lights.
l There were so many people ________________ the doctor's this morning.
m I saw Ann ________________ the bus stop.
n There's somebody ________________ the door. Can you go and see who it is?
o We lay ________________ the beach and enjoyed the sunshine.
p Is there anything interesting ________________ TV this evening?
q What time did you go ________________ bed last night?
r Tina's ________________ work. She'll be back at six.

3. Übersetzen Sie.

a Unsere Wohnung ist in der siebten Etage.
b Bist du auf dem Bild?
c Warum warst du gestern nicht in der Arbeit?
d Sie hatte ein schönes Poster an der Wand.
e Ich möchte am Meer leben.
f Er wohnt in [der][1] Amersham Road Nr. 309.

[1] Wörter in eckigen Klammern müssen nicht übersetzt werden.

TEST 5

Units 52–65

Wählen Sie die richtige Form.

Indirekte Rede

1. Tony ... he met Anna last week.
   a) said
   b) said, that

2. The man said he ... help.
   a) need
   b) needed

3. When I phoned, Ben said they ... supper.
   a) had
   b) were having

4. Robert ... that Emma was in hospital.
   a) said us
   b) told us

5. John said he ... a new bicycle.
   a) wanted
   b) would

6. They asked me if I ... anything about astronomy.
   a) did know
   b) knew

if-Sätze

7. ... I'm late, don't wait for me. Start without me.
   a) If
   b) When

8. Is it OK ... I park in the street overnight?
   a) if
   b) when

9. I ... if the train is late. Is that OK?
   a) phone
   b) will phone

10. If they ... too expensive, we can perhaps buy two of them.
    a) aren't
    b) won't be

11. What would you do if you ... a lot of money?
    a) won
    b) would win

12. If you ... me, you wouldn't ask me to do that.
    a) loved
    b) would love

13. I ... if I never saw him again!
    a) am not sorry
    b) wouldn't be sorry

Adjektiv und Adverb

14. It's one of my favourite restaurants. They always present the food so ... .
    a) beautiful
    b) beautifully

15. You don't have to do anything. It switches off ... .
    a) automatic
    b) automatically

16. Where did you learn to dance so ...?
    a) good
    b) well

17. Why is there so much traffic? This is ... unusual for a Monday evening.
    a) extreme
    b) extremely

18. The people here all work very … .
   a) ☐ hard
   b) ☐ hardly

19. She's younger … her husband.
   a) ☐ as
   b) ☐ than

20. Which is …: ice on the road or fog?
   a) ☐ badder
   b) ☐ worse

21. The designer watch isn't better, but it's … .
   a) ☐ expensiver
   b) ☐ more expensive

22. Ann is two years younger, but she is … her brother.
   a) ☐ as tall as
   b) ☐ so tall as

23. What is the … thing that has ever happened to you?
   a) ☐ most wonderful
   b) ☐ wonderfullest

some – any

24. Can I have … sugar, please?
   a) ☐ any
   b) ☐ some

25. I'm sorry, but I can't give you … details.
   a) ☐ any
   b) ☐ some

Präpositionen

26. I started work … Monday 1st July.
   a) ☐ at
   b) ☐ on

27. I find I can work better … night.
   a) ☐ at
   b) ☐ in

28. She left home … the age of 17.
   a) ☐ at
   b) ☐ in

29. My office is … the second floor.
   a) ☐ in
   b) ☐ on

30. We went … a concert last night. It was wonderful.
   a) ☐ in
   b) ☐ to

Vergleichen Sie nun Ihre Lösungen mit dem Schlüssel auf S. 165. Wenn Sie Aufgaben nicht richtig gelöst haben, wiederholen Sie noch einmal die betreffende Unit. Diese Tabelle zeigt Ihnen, auf welche Unit sich die einzelnen Aufgaben beziehen.

Aufgabe	Unit	Aufgabe	Unit
1	52	16	60
2	52	17	60
3	53	18	60
4	54	19	61
5	54	20	61
6	55	21	61
7	56	22	62
8	56	23	62
9	57	24	63
10	57	25	63
11	58	26	64
12	58	27	64
13	58	28	64
14	59	29	65
15	59	30	65

1

1 a eat; b likes; c finish; d plays; e watches; f read

2 a lives; b speaks; c teaches; d washes; e has; f drives

3 a open; b leaves, arrives; c know; d smokes, hate; e watch; f goes

4 a studies; b tries; c does; d finish; e like; f have

2

1 a don't smoke; b doesn't speak; c don't eat; d doesn't drink; e doesn't go; f don't open

2 a We don't go out in the week. b My husband doesn't speak Spanish. c It doesn't cost $50. d Mary doesn't live with her boyfriend. e They don't open on Sundays. f I don't have enough money.

3 a don't drink, drive; b says, doesn't want; c work, don't see, don't know; d don't take, don't think; e doesn't stop; f doesn't say, costs

4 a lives, doesn't speak; b has, doesn't work; c doesn't play, watches; d don't work; e don't want; f write, don't surf

3

1 a never arrives; b swims 500 m every morning; c sometimes watch; d wash my hair every day; e don't always come; f never help

2 a She always smiles at me. b We don't go to the sauna every week. c They don't always phone us before they come. d I often cook for friends on Sunday. e It never snows a lot here. f They don't have a holiday every year.

3 a I never drive very fast. b He drinks a glass of red wine every day. c We don't always buy a paper. d My daughter sometimes helps me. e The car doesn't always start first time. f Dave washes his car every Saturday.

4 a We never go swimming at the weekend. b I always get up very early. c My son listens to loud music every evening. d I don't often stay in hotels. e My colleague often goes to the cinema. f For lunch we usually eat / have salad.

4

1 a does; b do; c do; d does; e does; f do; g does; h does

2 a Where do you live? b What do you do? c Where do you (usually) go on holiday? d How do you travel? e How long do you stay? f What do you do there?

3 a What kind of foreign car does he drive? b What kind of dog do they have? c What kind of books do you write? d What kind of exotic food do you like? e What kind of instrument does he play? f What kind of card do you need (for Anita)?

4 a What does this word mean? b How often do you train? c Where do your parents live? d When do you get up? f Where does your son work?

5

1 a Do, do; b Does, doesn't; c Do, don't; d Does, doesn't; e Does, does; f Does, doesn't

2 *1. Teil: Individuelle Antworten mit* Yes, I do *oder* No, I don't.

2. Teil: a Does he / she like fish? b Does he / she speak French? c Does he / she play an instrument? d Does he / she live in a flat? e Does he / she listen to the radio much? f Does he / she travel a lot?

Individuelle Antworten mit Yes, he / she does *oder* No, he / she doesn't.
3 a Do you eat a big lunch? b Do you get up early? c Does she know his phone number? d Does she work very hard? e Does it cost much? f Do you do much sport?
4 a Do you live here? – Yes, I do. b Does Tom know the address? – Yes, he does. c Does she like roses? – Yes, she does. d Do they play tennis? – No, they don't. e Does the President / president speak German? – No, he doesn't.

6

1 a am / 'm finishing; b are / 're having; c is / 's playing; d am / 'm writing; e is / 's sitting; f are / 're waiting; g is / 's having; h is / 's ringing
2 b isn't working, is / 's playing; c aren't cooking, are / 're eating d am / 'm not watching, am / 'm doing; e aren't / 're not listening, are / 're looking; f aren't playing, are / 're sitting
3 a He is / He's relaxing at home. b He is / He's sitting in a chair. c He isn't / 's not watching TV. d He is / He's listening to music. e He is / He's talking on the telephone. f He isn't / 's not using a mobile phone.

7

1 a I am just finishing my supper. b The sun isn't shining today. c She's having a shower at the moment. d The children are just watching a video. e He's reading your fax now. f We aren't going on holiday this year.
2 b are just bringing; c is just telling; d am just making; e is just switching; f is just taking off
3 a Tina is / Tina's walking to work this week. b We are / We're eating a lot of salads at the moment. c I am not / I'm not using the computer now. d My husband is / My husband's doing a lot of sport at the moment. e We are / We're trying out a new producer in China at the moment. f We aren't / We're not going to the Hanover Fair this year.
4 a It is / It's just starting to rain. b We are / We're staying at home this evening. c My wife is / My wife's working very hard at the moment. d I am / 'm waiting for his answer now. e Someone is / Someone's using the copier at the moment. f We are / We're discussing the project this afternoon.

8

1 a Is; b is; c are; d am; e Are; f Is
2 *Individuelle Antworten mit* Yes, I am *oder* No, I'm not.
3 a Is she wearing a pullover? – No, she isn't. b Is Tim wearing jeans? – No, he isn't. c Is he carrying a bag? – Yes, he is. d Is Tina asking him a question? – Yes, she is. e Are Tim and Tina going to work? – No, they aren't. f Is Tim feeling happy? – No, he isn't.
4 a Why are you laughing? b What is your daughter studying? c Is Anja coming? – Yes, she is. d Are the children watching TV / television? – Yes, they are. e Is your wife working today? – No, she isn't. f What is he saying?

9

1 a never see; b am just listening; c usually phones; d are waiting; e isn't raining; f doesn't often happen
2 a watch; b is watching; c is talking; d is just watching; e plays; f does, watches
3 a aren't doing; b don't normally smoke;

c aren't making; d don't normally pay; e isn't working; f don't usually arrive
4 a Is Phil working; b do you go; c Do you often visit; d Is your boss travelling; e do you usually start; f are you doing

10

1 b Inflation is falling. c The temperature is dropping. d Our market share is increasing. e The population is growing. f Unemployment is going down.
2 b D, live; c V, is staying; d V, is studying; e D, teaches; f V, is making
3 a is shining; b are painting; c am learning, speaks; d are eating; e works, is working
4 a are you doing, Are you waiting; b do you read; c are you going; d do you get; e Do you speak

11

1 a thinks; b need; c doesn't want; d don't understand; e don't remember, Do you remember?
2 a want, don't know, depends on; b don't like, don't know; c Do you understand, don't understand; d belongs to, don't know
3 a are having; b have; c do the Smiths have; d is having; e do you have; f is having
4 a think; b think; c are thinking; d is thinking; e think; f Do you think, think
5 a am waiting, want, has; b are thinking, think; c is having, has; d have, need; e do you think, seems

Test 1

1a, 2a, 3b, 4a, 5b, 6b, 7a, 8a, 9a, 10a, 11b, 12b, 13b, 14a, 15a, 16a, 17a, 18a, 19b, 20b, 21a, 22b, 23a, 24a, 25b, 26a, 27b, 28a, 29b, 30b

12

1 a was; b was; c Were; d weren't; e weren't; f wasn't
2 a was; b was, were; c wasn't, was; d weren't, were; e was, wasn't, was; f were, weren't
3 a Were – Yes, I was. / No, I wasn't. b Was – Yes, it was. / No, it wasn't. c Was – Yes, it was. / No, it wasn't. d Was – Yes, it was. / No, it wasn't. e Were – Yes, they were. / No, they weren't. f Were – Yes, I was. / No, I wasn't.
4 a Where were you yesterday? Were you ill? b How was your holiday? / What was your holiday like? – It was great. c The weather and the hotel were both very good. d The journey was very long. It wasn't easy. e The parents weren't at home. The children were alone. f When was Angelo here? Was it last year?

13

1 a didn't stay; b tried; c planned; d didn't rain; e happened; f arrived
2 a lived; b started; c stopped; d studied; e phoned
3 a We didn't play mini-golf. b They didn't clean the windows. c Angela didn't plan the conference party. d I didn't order wine. e We didn't arrive together.
4 a wanted, didn't like; b enjoyed, didn't miss; c planned, visited; d started, hurried; e seemed, wasn't
5 a watched, didn't go; b asked, seemed; c didn't learn, played; d didn't plan it, happened; e tried, didn't want

14

1 a flew; b sat; c felt; d spoke; e didn't understand; f didn't do

2 a found, took, didn't want, gave; b didn't know, had, spoke, ate, had, didn't drink; c didn't pay, cost; d didn't do, wasn't, stayed, read, listened, watched, wrote; e came, met, had; f forgot, saw, told, said, knew
3 a lost, took; b fell, broke; c put, didn't do; d heard, saw; e bought, sat

15

1 a Did, didn't; b Did, did; c Did, didn't; d Did, did; e Did, didn't; f Did, did
2 a did you arrive; b did you park; c did you find out; d did you see; e did you do; f did you do
3 a Did you sleep; b Did you get up; c Did you watch; d Did you go out; e Did you stay; f Did you buy *Individuelle Antworten mit* Yes, I did *oder* No, I didn't.
4 a Did it rain yesterday? b How did it happen? c How did his parents find out? d Did you have a good journey? e How much did it cost?

16

1 a arrived; b lost; c left; d happened; e didn't meet; f didn't snow; g did you tell; h did this e-mail arrive
2 a I watched / didn't watch TV yesterday. b I travelled / didn't travel by train last week. c I started / didn't start to learn English two years ago. d I had / didn't have breakfast at 6.30 this morning. e I lived / didn't live here in 1999.
3 a I ate fish yesterday. b Ann gave a big party on 6th June. c We didn't have time on Friday. d The taxi didn't cost so much last time. e They didn't have a holiday in 2002. f The postman brought these two letters ten minutes ago.
4 a five days ago; b an / one hour ago; c three years ago; d a / one month ago; e ten minutes ago; f two weeks ago
5 a When did you arrive? b We bought the house four years ago. c Mr Smith died two days ago. d Ann and Ian married / got married in 2001. e I saw this film last year at the cinema.

17

1 a was talking; b was wearing; c were dancing; d were waiting; e were sitting; f were smoking
2 a It wasn't raining. The sun was shining! b He wasn't cooking. He was washing up. c I wasn't surfing. I was writing an e-mail! d They weren't working hard. They were talking. e She wasn't buying anything. She was just looking. f We weren't playing cards. We were watching football!
3 a were they laughing, was telling; b were you living, was working; c were you doing, was trying; d was she wearing, was going; e Were you waiting, was waiting; f Was David driving? – was sitting
4 a The birds were singing and the sun was shining. b He was interviewing the owner of the shop. c What were you doing at 8 o'clock? d The train was just leaving. e People were standing in the gangways. Some were sitting on the floor. f We were wearing our oldest things. We were working in the garden.

18

1 a was having, rang; b saw, was driving; c went, were waiting; d were having, came
2 a was having, arrived; b were eating, went; c exploded, were waiting; d was discussing, phoned; e was waiting, saw; f came, were having

3 a When we arrived, the sun was shining. b She was eating a sandwich when I brought / took her the fax. c I was cleaning my teeth when the postman came. d I took the post and locked the door. e I was reading the letter when my boss came in. f I read the letter and gave it to my boss.

19

1 a has; b haven't; c has; d seen; e done; f paid

2 a have accepted; b haven't answered; c have organized; d have missed; e has happened; f hasn't rained

3 a has lost; b have made; c haven't forgotten; d have drunk; e has brought; f have met

4 a I have spoken to my boss. b The children have learned / learnt to wait. c He hasn't paid the bill. d Angela has found a new flat. e Someone / -body has taken our parking space!

5 *Individuelle Antworten:* I've done / I haven't done a lot of work today. I've drunk / I haven't drunk alcohol today. I've driven / I haven't driven a car today. I've eaten / I haven't eaten a hot meal today. I've flown / I haven't flown today. I've heard/seen / I haven't heard/seen a plane today. I've made / I haven't made tea today. I've met / I haven't met a friend today. I've read / I haven't read a paper today. I've spoken / I haven't spoken English today. I've watched / I haven't watched TV today. I've written / I haven't written an e-mail today.

20

1 a Have, haven't; b Has, hasn't; c Has, has; d Have, haven't; e Have, have; f Have, have

2 a been; b tried; c bought; d spoken; e flown *Individuelle Antworten mit* No, I have never been / tried / bought / spoken / flown ... *oder* Yes, I did that ...

3 a Have you ever been – went, saw, were; b Have you ever bought – bought, paid; c Has Tony ever seen – wore, were; d Have we ever had – had, drove; e Has / Have this team ever won – won

4 a Have you ever been to Australia? b Last weekend we went to Paris. c Have you ever been to the USA? – Yes, I have. I went to Florida in 2002. d Ann has been to Canada. She went to Toronto two years ago.

21

1 a lately / recently; b yet; c already; d before

2 a haven't started yet; b have just finished; c has just stopped; d haven't found my keys yet; e have already spent; haven't seen her lately

3 a has done, before; b Have you told, yet; c has already arrived; d haven't had, lately / recently; e have seen, before; f have had, lately / recently; g Has Andy finished, yet

4 a went; b saw; c hasn't come; d did this letter arrive; e hasn't happened; f started, has lost; g Have they delivered, did they plan

22

1 a have been; b has bought; c have had; d have finished; e have had; f has eaten

2 a have moved, moved; b has gone, went; c have seen, saw; d haven't told, told; e sold, have sold; f has stopped, stopped

3 a *falsch, richtig ist* went; b *falsch, richtig ist* haven't been; c *richtig*; d *falsch, richtig ist* flew; e *falsch, richtig ist* have always lived; f *falsch, richtig ist* have never been to

4 a phoned / called / rang, has had; b worked, came; c have come, brought; d packed, haven't packed; e have been to, flew

23

1 a since; b for; c since; d since; e for; f for; g since; h for; i since; j for; k since; l since

2 a They have been friends for many years. *Sie sind seit vielen Jahren Freunde / befreundet.* b We have known each other since we were 15. *Wir kennen uns, seit wir 15 waren.* c My mother has been in hospital for more than two months. *Meine Mutter ist / liegt seit mehr als zwei Monaten im Krankenhaus.* d Mrs Bolton has worked here for seven years. *Mrs Bolton arbeitet seit sieben Jahren hier.* e Peter has been in the Peking office since 1st April. *Peter ist seit dem 1. April im Pekinger Büro.* f Bonnie has had a terrible cold since the weekend. *Bonnie hat eine furchtbare Erkältung seit dem Wochenende.* g I have watched this programme every week since the beginning. *Ich schaue diese Sendung jede Woche seit Anbeginn / Ich habe diese Sendung … (an)geschaut.*

3 a has been, since; *Sarah macht seit letzter Woche Diät.* b have been, for; *Mein Partner / Meine Partnerin und ich sind nun seit drei Jahren zusammen.* c have lived, for; *Sie wohnen seit über einem Jahr dort.* d have known, since; *Ich kenne Ellen, seit(dem) wir zusammen im Kindergarten waren.* e has happened, since; *Das ist dreimal passiert, seit sie das neue System installiert haben.* f Since, have used; *Seitdem / Seit damals benutzen wir eine andere Route / einen anderen Weg.* g haven't heard, for; *Ich habe seit Monaten nichts mehr von Barry gehört.* h haven't watched, for; *Die Kinder haben seit über einer Woche nicht ferngesehen.* i have made, for; *Sie machen seit Jahren Geld damit.*

4 a We have known Peter Hollis since 1999. b Mrs Thomas has worked for us for six months. c He has been ill since Sunday. d Mary's husband has been dead for several years. e We have known for a long time about this organization / … about this organization for a long time. f I have had a headache since this morning.

24

1 a How long have you known Mr Ling? b How long has Alex been ill now? c How long have Peter and Jill been married now? d How long have you known this? e How long have they had this problem? f How long have you been back from your holiday?

2 *Individuelle Antworten* c I've worked where I work now … d I have had … e I have used this book …

3 a How long has he had that / it / a VW Beetle? b How long have you known her / Annabelle? c How long have you used that / it / a courier service? d How long have they had it / one / a dog? e How long have you lived there / on an island? f How long has he worked there / in a hotel?

4 a I have been here all morning. b Tina has been ill all week. c How long have you known Mr Jameson? d How long has he driven this / that old Ford? e How long have you had this flat? f I have known this place all my life.

25

1 a has been doing; b has been talking; c has it been snowing; d has been training for

2 a Tina has been waiting for 45 minutes. b She has been standing in the cold all the

time. c She has been getting more and more angry. d Tim has been sitting in a pub since 5.30. e He has been talking to an old friend. f They have been drinking beer.

3 a How long has she been reading? She has been reading for two hours. b How long has he been studying? He has been studying for 35 minutes. c How long has he been cleaning his car? He has been cleaning his car for 40 minutes. d How long have they been playing tennis? They have been playing tennis for 1 hour.

4 a How long have you been waiting? b She has been working on the project since August. c Mrs Smith's dog has been barking all evening. d How long have we been trying to reach him? e It has been raining all week. f We have been driving for five hours.

Test 2

1a, 2b, 3b, 4a, 5a, 6b, 7b, 8b, 9b, 10b, 11b, 12a, 13b, 14b, 15b, 16b, 17a, 18b, 19a, 20a, 21b, 22b, 23b, 24b, 25b, 26b, 27b, 28a, 29b, 30b

26

1 a used to; b didn't use to; c Did he use to; d did you use to; e used to phone; f didn't use to

2 a used to drive; b used to live; c used to work; d used to drink; e used to have; f used to play; g used to be

3 a We used to park in Castle Street. b I didn't use to like Sonia's husband. c Families used to have only one television (set). d We used to order by letter. e Salmon used to be an expensive fish. f Where did you use to live?

4 *Individuelle Antworten mit* I used to … *oder* I didn't use to …

27

1 a had already left; b had already cooked; c had arrived; d had fallen; e had worked; f had forgotten; g had reserved

2 a They had seen two accidents. b They had stood in a traffic jam for two hours. c They had had a breakdown. d They had lost their way twice. e They had left the hotel address at home.

3 a I hadn't cooked that before. b We hadn't eaten that before. c I hadn't met them before. d I hadn't been to one before. e I hadn't had one before. f I hadn't worn it before.

4 a Tim's plane had already landed. b But someone / somebody had already informed her. c But we hadn't seen the film. d He had forgotten his passport. e She had won €500 on the lottery. f I hadn't slept much.

28

1 a are going to stay; b is going to wait; c is going to sell; d is going to take; e are going to win; f am going to ask; g am going to make; h is going to phone; i is going to drive; j are going to stay

2 a I'm not going to make it. b I'm not going to offer. c I'm not going to tell you. d I'm not going to do it. e I'm not going to agree to that.

3 a Who are you going to invite? b What are you going to wear? c Which film are you going to see? d Where are you going to park? e What are you going to give her (for her birthday)?

4 a It is going to rain. b The train is going to leave. c She is going to have a baby. d The bus is going to stop.

29

1 a is coming; b am meeting; c are going; d is giving; e are you doing; f are you leaving; g are we meeting; h are you going

2 a she is going to the cinema with Jill. b she is going to the dentist (at 10 o'clock). c she is cooking for Mike's birthday party. d she is having lunch with her mum. e she is working from 3 o'clock (in the afternoon) to / till 9 o'clock (in the evening). f she is playing tennis with Adrian. g she is going to the sauna. h she is working from 9 o'clock (in the morning) to / till 4 o'clock (in the afternoon).

3 a Where is the club committee meeting tomorrow evening? b When are we playing next Saturday? c What time are we seeing the Smiths next Sunday? d When is Andrew fetching these chairs? e What day is your mother arriving? f When are they delivering the new fax machine?

30

1 a wants; b will be; c don't want to; d will see; e will miss; f wants to

2 a I'll put you through. b I'll show you your room. c I think Mark will phone later this evening. d Quick, or they'll close. e Mrs Wilkins will be here very soon. f I'm afraid he'll fail his final exam.

3 a will be; b will enjoy; c will snow; d won't know; e won't be; f will they do, will they go

4 a You'll see: we'll win on Saturday. b We'll know more tomorrow. c Mr Baker will call back tomorrow. d Tomorrow he'll feel much better. e Sally will be here in five minutes. f In future I'll be more careful. It won't happen again.

31

1 a I'll wait; b we'll find out; c Richard will be; d the police will find; e we'll miss; f it won't rain

2 a I'll ask him. b I'll carry it for you. c I'll eat it. d I'll open the window. e I'll make some coffee. f I'll wait (for him).

3 a are going to stay; b 'll buy; c 'll eat; d are going to give; e 'll do; f am going to do

4 a I'll help you. b I think we'll lose on Saturday. c I'll show you the way. d I'll have the fish, please. e I'll send her an e-mail. f No problem, I'll pay.

32

1 a is sold; b was paid; c will be delivered; d were ordered; e must be collected; f aren't accepted

2 a is spoken; b is drunk; c is sold; d are asked; e am known; f are given; g is made

3 a The thief was seen. b Two men were arrested last night. c Over 50000 CDs were sold on the first day. d The book was written in 1928. e Over 3000 civilians were killed. f The new museum was opened last year.

4 a can / may be left; b must be paid; c will be informed; d can be ordered; e must be parked; f can be used again / can be reused

33

1 a has been stolen; b is being painted; c has been paid; d is being built; e are being sent out; f has been fired

2 a is being developed; b is being built; c is being repaired; d is being interviewed; e are being treated; f is being said

3 a All the tickets have been sold. b The

keys have been found. c We have been informed. d Coffee has already been made. e The whole restaurant has been booked. f I have been asked to help.
4 a has been stolen; b is being cleaned; c haven't been invited; d is being filmed; e has been sold; f is being delivered

34

1 a The match was won by Bayern Munich. b Who was this book written by? c The ceremony was watched by millions on TV. d His father was killed by a terrorist. e Who was this picture painted by? f Who were you invited by?
2 a This fax was sent by Tony. b Our cat was fed by a neighbour. c The hotel was chosen by my secretary. d The Italian course is taught by an Australian. e The thief was seen by two boys. f Our computer was installed by my son.
3 a Who was President Kennedy killed by? b Who was the first computer made by? c Who was the letter signed by? d Who were you invited by? e Who was the gold medal won by? f Who were you informed by?
4 a Who was he informed by? b Who are you (being) paid by? c The party was organized by the parents. d English is spoken by millions of people. e I am always woken up by my son. f The book was written by an American.

35

1 a Sorry, who did you meet? b Sorry, who did you visit? c Sorry, who did the police arrest? d Sorry, who did you ask the way? e Sorry, who did Ann see? f Sorry, who did you teach to swim?
2 a What does this cost? b What do you think? c What do you serve with this fish? d What do people without a car do? e What do you do at weekends? f What does the thermometer say?
3 a Who did you meet (at the party)? b Who paid? c Who arrived last? d Who planned the whole thing? e Who won? f Who did Angela phone?
4 a What do you want? b What does this pullover cost? c Who phoned / called / rang yesterday evening / last night? d Who do you know here? e What happens in the film? f Who did you meet at the party last weekend?

36

1 a Who do you work for? b What are you interested in? c Where do you come from? d What do you believe in? e Which part of the country do you live in? f What are you especially good at?
2 a Which hotel did you stay in? b Who did you go sailing with? c What did you drive around in? d What did you send postcards of? e What did you look for? f Who did you buy souvenirs for?
3 a Who are you going on holiday with? b What was the boss so angry about? c What were you afraid of? d Who did Tom play tennis with yesterday? e Who does old Mrs Lacy live with?
4 a Who is he speaking / talking to? b What are they talking about? c What are you waiting for? d Who are you writing to? e Which flat are they looking at today?

37

1 a doesn't he; b is she; c am I; d were you; e didn't they; f haven't we
2 a are you; b am I; c aren't they; d isn't it; e were they; f aren't you

3 a wasn't; b does; c haven't; d has; e will; f don't
4 a don't you; b doesn't it; c doesn't he; d don't they; e didn't we; f didn't I

38

1 a will be able to; b can speak; c couldn't; d been able to; e will you; f can do it
2 *Individuelle Antworten mit* I could ... *oder* I couldn't ...
3 a have been able to find; b won't be able to come; c haven't been able to phone; d will you be able to tell; e haven't been able to repair; f Has Tony been able to help
4 a We'll be able to let you know next week. b Bernd's mother is American. He can speak two languages, German and English. c Have you been able to speak / talk to your parents? d We could see / were able to see more than 100 kilometres. e I can't speak Spanish. Can you understand what the man wants? f Ben will be able to come, but I work on Saturday(s).

39

1 a doesn't have to; b don't have to; c don't have to; d don't have to; e don't have to; f doesn't have to
2 a We don't have to book. b You don't have to be very athletic to play golf. c She doesn't have to ask Tim for help. d He doesn't have to go shopping now. e I don't have to paint the flat when I move out. f We don't have to go out.
3 a mustn't; b needn't; c don't have to; d needn't; e mustn't; f needn't
4 a I mustn't forget (it). b We don't have to / needn't listen to music. c You don't have to / needn't help me. d He doesn't have to / needn't drive. e You mustn't tell anyone / anybody. f It doesn't always have to / needn't always be caviar.

40

1 a don't have to; b had to; c have to; d has had to sell; e Do customers have; f had to
2 b We'll have to book a taxi the evening before. c We'll have to go to bed early. d We'll have to get up at 4.30. e We'll have to leave home at 5.15. f We'll have to have breakfast at the airport.
3 a don't have to pay; b doesn't have to give; c didn't have to wait; d didn't have to do; e do you have to start work; f did your friends have to pay; g did he have to do; h Did you have to look
4 a The passengers had to wait 90 minutes. b You will have to take a day's holiday. c Do you have to work every weekend? – No, only two weekends in the month. d When do we have to pay? e When will we have to get up? f You will have to ask the boss. I can't decide that.

41

1 a himself; b him; c me; d myself; e themselves; f them
2 a They want to make themselves useful. b We paid for ouselves. c He taught himself to swim. d This is a question I ask myself all the time! e She only thinks about herself. f Have you bought yourselves new clothes?
3 a yourself; b himself; c ourselves; d yourselves; e themselves; f myself
4 a I sometimes ask myself why he did it / that. b They built the house themselves. c May I introduce myself? d I can't / cannot help you. You must / have to help yourself. e He said to himself: This is my last cigarette.

f We have a club and call ourselves "The Oldies".

42

1 a each other; b –; c each other; d meet; e each other; f concentrate
2 a himself; b each other; c –; d yourself, –; e –; f herself
3 a complain; b meet; c get divorced; d wonder; e hurry; f feel
4 a When was that? Can you remember? b How do you feel? c I can't / cannot concentrate. d Our world has changed. e Why are you arguing? f Our son has fallen in love again.

43

1 a who; b who; c that; d that; e which; f who
2 a who; b which; c who; d which; e who; f who
3 a The letter which / that came this morning didn't have a stamp. b The ball which / that landed in our garden belonged to our neighbours' children. c The woman who took my name knows you. d The car which / that overtook us didn't have any lights. e The man who came to the door said that he was a detective. f The girl who served us was only about 13.
4 a Are people who smoke thinner? b I like flowers that smell. c He is someone / somebody who needs a lot of sleep. d A millionaire is someone / somebody who has a lot of money. e I need a flat which / that is big but doesn't cost much.

44

1 a What is the CD you are listening to? b Dave is the person I played tennis with last weekend. c We have some friends who moved to California last year. d The rocks you are looking at are some of the oldest in the world.
2 a –; b which; c who; d –; e –; f who
3 a Did you find the book you were looking for? b This is the house I lived in as a child. c Where is the magazine I left on the sofa? d Who was the woman you were speaking to? e Josie is a friend I was at school with.
4 a The man I have the information from is an expert. b My colleague has a dog which / that sings. c The people we met there were all very poor. d Is this / that the key you are looking for? e I don't know the woman John is speaking / talking to. f The present I have for my parents is very big / large.

Test 3

1b, 2a, 3a, 4a, 5a, 6b, 7b, 8b, 9b, 10b, 11b, 12b, 13a, 14a, 15a, 16a, 17b, 18b, 19a, 20b, 21a, 22a, 23a, 24a, 25a, 26a, 27a, 28b, 29b, 30a

45

1 a getting; b waiting; c smoking; d making; e swimming; f writing
2 a *Individuelle Antworten mit* living / working / getting up / wearing / writing / eating / going / cooking …
3 a Would you mind repeating that? b Would you mind leaving us alone? c Would you mind switching off your mobile phone? d Would you mind moving your bag? e Would you mind not smoking? f Would you mind not parking here?
4 a Can you imagine being rich? b I really enjoy listening to her. c I tried to avoid looking at it. d We don't want to risk breaking it. e Practise saying that in English. f I suggest waiting till prices fall again.

46

1 a having; b to see; c to eat; d to do; e to come; f to do

2 a Where would you like to go today? b Would you prefer to stay at home this evening? c What would you like to see? d Which programme would you prefer to watch? e Would you like to try a piece of Christmas Cake? f What would you prefer to do today?

3 would love to sleep; want to sleep; always avoid sleeping; suggested sleeping; enjoy sleeping; hate sleeping / to sleep; prefer not to sleep; have given up sleeping; have stopped sleeping; never like sleeping / to sleep; managed to sleep; decided to sleep; hoped to sleep; love sleeping / to sleep; planned to sleep; would like to sleep

4 a Tim (has) offered to help. b I would love to visit New Zealand. c Can you imagine living in New Zealand? d I suggest taking a taxi. e We would hate to pay more. f It has stopped raining. We can go.

47

1 a starting; b coming; c cooking; d buying; e waking; f inviting

2 a People here are used to driving long distances to work. b I am really looking forward to finishing this project. c No more, thanks. I'm not used to drinking so much. d Andy is looking forward to surfing again in the summer.

3 a for being; b on repairing; c for looking; d of / about being; e like having; f about making

4 a We have always dreamed / dreamt of visiting Tibet. b It isn't / It's not worth waiting. c Do you feel like seeing a film? d Have you ever thought about / of buying a flat? e I'm looking forward to going on holiday. f My son isn't / is not used to working hard.

48

1 a coming; b growing; c forgetting; d waking; e losing; f listening

2 a I hate the idea of losing an old friend. b Do we have an alternative to accepting this offer? c My grandfather had the habit of smoking Havana cigars in the bath. d We have the choice of paying now or later. e The thought of swimming in the sea every day is wonderful. f I'm not interested in playing chess.

3 a at drawing; b of falling and breaking; c for leaving; d of going; e about meeting; f for writing

4 a I have a special reason for inviting David Waters. b You risk / are in danger of missing the last train. c David is so bad at planning. d We were tired of / fed up with meeting the same people. e I'm not interested in meeting Michael Schumacher. f She has the habit of / is in the habit of phoning / calling / ringing (up) in the middle of the night.

49

1 a leaving; b making, drinking; c asking; d sitting; e telling

2 a How / What about asking Phil? b How / What about going to bed early? c How / What about eating out at that new restaurant? d How / What about buying her a CD? e How / What about taking a boat on the river? f How / What about phoning and asking her?

3 a Do something instead of just sitting there. b I said it without thinking. c John sent an e-mail before going offline. d You can find out what Ann would like for her birthday by asking Tony. e I always do exer-

cises in bed before getting up. f You can save a lot of money by checking prices on the internet.
4 a Instead of waiting for Tim, let's ask Desmond. b The man left the restaurant without paying. c You open the mail by clicking here. d Tony learned Spanish by reading Spanish comics. e How / What about staying at home this evening / tonight?

50

1 a I want Joe to phone New York. b I want Lisa to do the photocopying. c I want Peter to make some coffee. d I want Ann to send a fax to Chicago. e I want Doris to book a table for lunch. f I want William to book a hotel for me.
2 a I want you to go now. b We would like you to stay the night. c Would you like me to help with those bags? d The boss wants someone to work this weekend. e My partner would like us to get married. f They don't want us to pay now.
3 a My aunt advised me to take warm clothes. b They allowed me to take photos. c They invited me to stay and have dinner. d Ann's friend taught me to surf. e She asked me to wait in the foyer. f My friend helped me to install the program.
4 a I want you to help me. b We don't want the children to hear (it). c Would you like me to translate the text? d I want you to wait for me. e Would you like me to make coffee? f We would like you to come with us to London.

51

1 a use; b not to pay; c stand up; d not to go out; e to expect; f told
2 a The teacher told the children to be quiet. b Will you tell Ben to make some extra copies, please? c The doctor told me to give up smoking. d Can you tell Ann to phone home, please? e We warn tourists not to take too much cash with them. f I warned you not to go swimming so soon after that big lunch.
3 a let; b made; c let; d make; e made; f let
4 a I warned you not to drink too much of the wine. b I won't let you go till / until you apologize. c My colleague told me not to disturb the boss. d I won't let you pay. You are my guest today. e Tell your friend to come in. f He made his secretary work till / until 10 o'clock in the evening.

Test 4

1a, 2b, 3b, 4b, 5a, 6b, 7a, 8b, 9b, 10b, 11b, 12b, 13b, 14b, 15b, 16a, 17a, 18a, 19a, 20a, 21a, 22a, 23a, 24a, 25a, 26b, 27a, 28a, 29a, 30a

52

1 a *keine*; b *keine*; c Tina said, "It's time to get up." d The ticket collector said, "Tickets please." e My boss said, "What a terrible day!" f *keine*
2 a (that) she felt cold; b (that) they were too early; c (that) he needed more time; d (that) the situation didn't look good; e (that) he / she didn't like travelling at night; f (that) he wasn't ready; g (that) he / she didn't know the answer; h (that) he didn't speak German
3 a you were thirsty; b you said you wanted to go out; c you said it was easy; d you said it was cheap; e you said you had a key; f you said the water was nice and warm
4 a My husband said whisky was better than wine. b The boss said I was overqualified for the job. c But you said you liked short hair.

d My daughter said that she didn't want to go on holiday with us. e Tony said the dog didn't bite. f My friends said I looked like a ghost.

53

1 a was just reading; b couldn't drive me to the airport; c wouldn't invite; d had sent; e would bring; f might go
2 a she couldn't find her keys; b Tina was learning Chinese; c they would need some extra chairs; d it wasn't raining; e he'd phone the travel agent; f had lost his passport; g they had bought a caravan
3 a Margie said she had written the invitations. b Mark said he would buy the wine. c Sheila said she could borrow some chairs. d Philip said he would make a curry. e Mary said she had booked the band. f Anita said she was trying to book a clown.
4 a The man said he would call back later. b The customer said he couldn't pay because he didn't have enough money. c Gregor said he had done his best. d The woman said she was waiting for a phone call. e His secretary said he was speaking / talking on the other phone. f Tom said I could take his car.

54

1 a told me; b said; c told you; d hadn't played; e would phone; f would find out
2 a said; b say; c told; d say; e tell; f tell
3 a that the / his / her food was cold; b they had arrived safely; c a hotel room in London would be very expensive; d that he would pay me back when we got home; e she had found the perfect job; f (that) it was raining again
4 a He told his teacher that he had forgotten his homework. b I said that I wasn't hungry. c You promised me that you would deliver on Friday. d I said that I didn't have time. e I thought I had shut / closed the window. f We told him that he was too old for the job.

55

1 a liked; b could; c my report was; d when the film started; e asked Tom if he; f knew
2 b if / whether anyone had called the police; c if / whether the road was blocked; d if / whether I had given First Aid; e what had happened; f who saw / had seen the accident; g who was going to pay for the repair; h how many people were hurt
3 a how old I was; b if / whether I spoke English; c how long I had been in my present job; d what I hoped to earn; e if / whether I would be prepared to work at weekends; f how I heard / had heard about the job

56

1 a if; b When; c If; d phone; e see; f feel
2 a if; b If; c when; d If; e When; f If
3 a When the eggs are ready; b If we need more money; c If that policeman speaks English; d When I feel strong enough; e If you have time; f When Mr Smith arrives
4 a When you go this evening, please leave the light on. b If I'm not here / there, try again later. c Bring Tony if he has time. d When we have our new flat, we'll give a big party. e If the wine costs more than 10 euros, don't buy it. f When we get home, I'll make something to eat.

57

1 a arrives; b speak; c don't leave; d says; e is; f will

2 a If it's too expensive, we won't go. b I'll ask Donna if I see her. c It won't be easy if our best player is ill. d He won't get the job if he doesn't dress better for the interview. e What will you do if they say 'no'? f She will tell Adrian if she finds out more.
3 a If you drink this, you'll feel better. b If I don't like it, I'll order something else. c We'll keep it here for you if you don't want to take it with you now. d If you don't tell him soon, he'll find out from someone else. e It won't be a problem if you ask nicely. f If the phone rings, I'll answer it.
4 a If you go to bed now, you'll feel better tomorrow. b If I have enough money, I'll buy champagne. c I'll make the sandwiches if you want. d If you want, you can sleep here. e If it happens again, will you call / phone the police? f If we don't work faster, we won't be finished at 12 o'clock.

58

1 a was; b saw; c would leave; d owned; e offered; f didn't do
2 a would save; b saved; c went; d flew; e bought, would try; f was, would start
3 a If you worked harder, you would earn more money. b If he went to bed earlier, he wouldn't be so tired in the morning. c If you knew the name of the street, it would help. d If you found a job in Australia or the USA, would you go?
4 a If I had more money, I would take a bigger / larger flat. b If I was younger, I would try bungee jumping. c If I knew the answer, I would tell you. d If you asked Ann, she could help you. e It would be better if you didn't ask the boss today.

59

1 a nice; b clearly; c angrily; d dangerous; e slowly; f impossible
2 a regularly; b easily; c carefully; d politely; e automatically; f heavily
3 a big; b quietly; c slowly; d quick; e wildly; f thirsty; g stupidly; h automatically; i suddenly; j drunk; k simply; l probably; m politely
4 a Helga is the perfect secretary. b I (have) slept badly. c Are you happy in your new job? d It was a bad hotel. e The children (have) behaved perfectly. f The winner smiled / was smiling happily.

60

1 a well; b good; c hard; d extremely; e late; f hardly
2 a good, well; b good, well; c well, good; d well, good; e well, good; f well, well
3 a lately; b hard; c extremely; d hardly; e awfully; f terribly
4 a You sing very well and very beautifully. b My boss drives fast. He drives dangerously. c I know London well. d Tony goes to bed late and gets up early. e The weather was unusually warm. f Emma is playing very well.

61

1 a richer; b bigger; c more exclusive; d than; e worse; f happier
2 c harder; d quicker; e more interesting; f more important; g more famous; h worse; i crazier; j easier; k more difficult; l heavier; m thinner; n more careful; o better
3 a The plane is faster than the train. The train is slower than the plane. b Steak is more expensive than salmon. Salmon is

cheaper than steak. c Football is more boring than tennis. Tennis is more interesting than football. d Monday is worse than Friday. Friday is better than Monday.
4 a I am taller than you. b This restaurant is much more expensive than McDonald's. c The traffic yesterday was worse than today. d This problem is easier to solve. e A live concert is more exciting than a CD. f Who was more surprised – you or your boss?

62
1 a the most boring; b the best; c the hottest; d the worst; e the luckiest; f the most interesting
2 a The weather today is as warm as yesterday. b The weather today isn't as bad as yesterday. c Jack isn't as tall as Tony. d The Excelsior is as exclusive as the Bristol. e Steel isn't as hard as a diamond. f Going by train is as fast as going by plane.
3 a than b as; c than; d as; e as; f than
4 a Yesterday was the hottest day of the year. b The years in London were the happiest of my life. c He wears / is wearing the same shoes as you. d The price isn't as important as the quality. e Monday is the worst day of the week.

63
1 a I haven't read any of her books. b There aren't any interesting programmes on TV tonight. c We don't have any contacts in Sweden. d Tony didn't make any notes. e We don't need any batteries. f I won't see any old friends.
2 a any; b any interesting programmes; c have any contacts in Sweden; d make any notes; e need any batteries; meet any old friends
3 a make some sandwiches; b make some tea; c look for some photos; d Shall I open some windows? e Shall I phone some friends? f Shall I buy some flowers?
4 a some; b some; c any; d any; e any; f some; g any

64
1 a in ... at; b at ... in; c on; d at; e next; f on; g at; h last
2 a on; b on; c on; d at; e in; f at; g at; h at; i in; j at; k at; l at; m in; n on; o at; p on; q in; r at
3 a on, at, in; b At, in; c At, on; d at, in; e on, at, in; f –
4 a We are flying on Sunday morning at half past five. b I work at night. c Last Sunday I was in London. d I don't have any time at the moment. e Tony's father has died – at the age of 58. f What are you doing on your birthday?

65
1 a to; b in; c in; d at ... at; e on; f on
2 a in; b by; c on; d at; e on; f to; g in; h at; i at; j at; k at; l at; m at; n at; o on; p on; q to; r at
3 a Our flat is on the seventh floor. b Are you in the picture? c Why weren't you at work yesterday? d She had a nice poster on the wall. e I would like to live by the sea. f He lives at (no.) 309 Amersham Road.

Test 5
1a, 2b, 3b, 4b, 5a, 6b, 7a, 8a, 9b, 10a, 11a, 12a, 13b, 14b, 15b, 16b, 17b, 18a, 19b, 20b, 21b, 22a, 23a, 24b, 25a, 26b, 27a, 28a, 29b, 30b

Liste unregelmäßiger Verben

Grundform	Vergangenheitsform	Partizip Perfekt	
be	was/were	been	*sein*
become	became	become	*werden*
begin	began	begun	*beginnen*
break	broke	broken	*(zer)brechen*
bring	brought	brought	*bringen*
build	built	built	*bauen*
buy	bought	bought	*kaufen*
catch	caught	caught	*fangen, erwischen*
choose	chose	chosen	*(aus)wählen*
come	came	come	*kommen*
cost	cost	cost	*kosten*
cut	cut	cut	*schneiden*
do	did	done	*tun, machen*
drink	drank	drunk	*trinken*
drive	drove	driven	*fahren*
eat	ate	eaten	*essen*
fall	fell	fallen	*fallen*
feel	felt	felt	*(sich) (an)fühlen*
fight	fought	fought	*kämpfen*
find	found	found	*finden*
fly	flew	flown	*fliegen*
forbid	forbade	forbidden	*verbieten*
forget	forgot	forgotten	*vergessen*
freeze	froze	frozen	*(ge)frieren*
get	got	got	*bekommen*
give	gave	given	*geben*
go	went	gone	*gehen*
grow	grew	grown	*wachsen*
hang	hung	hung	*hängen*
have	had	had	*haben*
hear	heard	heard	*hören*
hold	held	held	*halten*
hurt	hurt	hurt	*wehtun*
keep	kept	kept	*weiter (tun)*
know	knew	known	*wissen, kennen*
lay	laid	laid	*legen*
lead	led	led	*führen, leiten*
leave	left	left	*(hinter)lassen; abfahren*
lend	lent	lent	*(aus)leihen*
let	let	let	*lassen*
lie	lay	lain	*liegen*

Grundform	Vergangenheitsform	Partizip Perfekt	
lose	lost	lost	*verlieren*
make	made	made	*machen*
mean	meant	meant	*bedeuten; meinen*
meet	met	met	*treffen*
pay	paid	paid	*(be)zahlen*
put	put	put	*stellen, stecken, legen*
read	read	read	*lesen*
ride	rode	ridden	*reiten; fahren*
ring	rang	rung	*anrufen; klingeln*
rise	rose	risen	*(an-, auf)steigen*
run	ran	run	*laufen*
say	said	said	*sagen*
see	saw	seen	*sehen*
sell	sold	sold	*verkaufen*
send	sent	sent	*senden*
shake	shook	shaken	*schütteln*
shine	shone	shone	*scheinen*
shoot	shot	shot	*(er)schießen*
show	showed	shown	*zeigen*
shut	shut	shut	*schließen*
sing	sang	sung	*singen*
sink	sank	sunk	*sinken, versenken*
sit	sat	sat	*sitzen*
sleep	slept	slept	*schlafen*
speak	spoke	spoken	*sprechen*
spend	spent	spent	*verbringen; ausgeben*
stand	stood	stood	*stehen*
steal	stole	stolen	*stehlen*
stick	stuck	stuck	*stecken; kleben*
swim	swam	swum	*schwimmen*
take	took	taken	*nehmen; dauern*
teach	taught	taught	*lehren, unterrichten*
tear	tore	torn	*reißen*
tell	told	told	*erzählen, sagen*
think	thought	thought	*denken*
throw	threw	thrown	*werfen*
understand	understood	understood	*verstehen*
wake	woke	woken	*wecken*
wear	wore	worn	*tragen*
win	won	won	*gewinnen*
write	wrote	written	*schreiben*

Die Zahlen verweisen auf das entsprechende Kapitel.